Soft Toys
Piece-by-Piece
STEP-BY-STEP INSTRUCTIONS

4/95

MILNER CRAFT SERIES

Soft Toys
Piece-by-Piece
STEP-BY-STEP INSTRUCTIONS

JANETTE ZAPIRAIN

SALLY MILNER PUBLISHING

First published in 1993 by
Sally Milner Publishing Pty Ltd
558 Darling Street
Rozelle NSW 2039 Australia

Design by Kerrilyn O'Donnell
Photography by Andre Martin
Typeset in Australia by Asset Typesetting Pty Ltd
Printed in Australia by Impact Printing

National Library of Australia
Cataloguing-in-Publication data:

Zapirain, Janette.
    Soft toys piece-by-piece.

    ISBN 1 86351 115 6.

    1. Soft toy making. I. Title. (Series : Milner craft series).

745.5924

CONTENTS

INTRODUCTION

DEDICATION AND ACKNOWLEDGEMENTS

This book would not have been possible without the encouragement, support and prayers of friends and family.

Special thanks go to four special people. To my husband, Tony, thanks for giving and forgiving — for 'giving' me time off from farm duties and for 'forgiving' my tiredness, bad moods and many complaints, especially those related to our very 'humble' house and the 'terrible mess' I made in it. To my daughters, Jodi (6½) and Samantha (5), who often found it frustrating that Mummy was so busy trying to 'get the book finished'. To my youngest baby girl, Rebecca (18 months), I hope I have not missed too much of your growing up. Rebecca 'loved' all the toys and would have happily played with the headless bodies and bodyless heads, if she were allowed.

Special thanks to my mum, Thelma, who on two occasions travelled the long distance from Nowra to look after the girls while I typed or did some sewing. Thanks also to my mother-in-law, Terry, for the loan of her old typewriter and also for the use of her electricity (occasionally) when I was in Dorrigo. This was very much appreciated as we have no electricity except that generated (only when absolutely necessary), by one of two small generators, one of which is borrowed.

Last, but definitely not least, thanks and praise to God for the talents He has given me. I could not have done anything at all without His inspiration.

INTRODUCTION

The toy designs in this book were developed because I got tired of making toys that were all the same. I wanted to be able to use the pattern over and over again, yet get a different result each time. Thus, the patterns are what I call 'mix and match', 'multiple choice' patterns. This means that even though only one set of basic instructions is given, such as for a Butterfly, a Bird and a Big Cat, more than one of each type of toy can be made.

I have tried to make the toys as true to life as is possible using a flat piece of fabric. Some of the toys, the Butterflies and Birds, can be made to move and are called 'finger action' toys. Children and adults alike enjoy playing with or just admiring these toys.

The patterns can be adapted according to your needs. Change the colours or use the designs as ideas for other projects. For example, the Butterfly designs can be used as motifs for quilts, pillows, sloppy joes or T-shirts. Three or more Butterflies could be hung as a mobile.

Method of Working

As you look through the book you will notice that the toys become a little harder to make, with the Big Cats taking the most time. All the instructions are given step-by-step and piece-by-piece, with accompanying illustrations, so that you can *read* as well as *see* what to do.

Always *pin* and *sew* following the illustration, reversing the whole procedure if a matching pair is needed. Follow the preliminary joining procedure and accompanying illustrations provided in the pattern section for those toys that require some joining before following the basic instructions.

Always use pins and tack when directed: do not rely on your ability to hold the fabric in place — remove the pins as you come to them. Sewing without pins may be successful when dressmaking, but with a small toy, a slip or shift in the fabric can cause uneven joining and an out-of-shape toy.

Except when stated otherwise, the *right* sides of the fabric should face each other when joining pieces together.

The seam allowance for each toy is given in the relevant pattern section.

The methods and techniques described are those that I have found the most successful. If they are different to the methods you have learnt or discovered, please feel free to use your own methods, *after* you have tried mine. Happy sewing ...

GLOSSARY OF STITCHES

Legend:

Right side of fabric

Wrong side of fabric

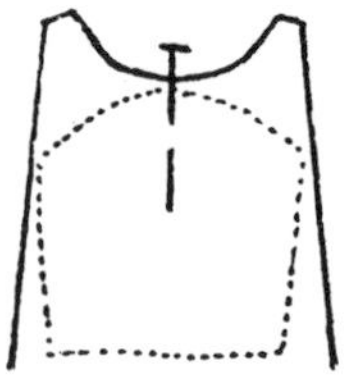

Dotted line shows obscured shape, underneath

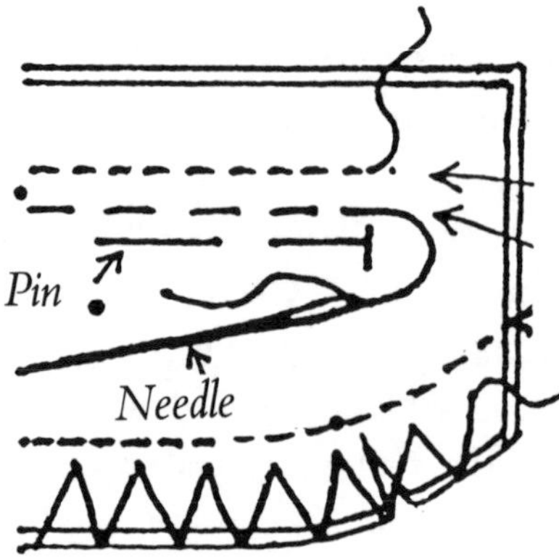

Raw edges even

Straight machine stitch

Hand tacking

Thread tied and cut

Edges overcast with machine zig zag

Curve clipped

Pin

Needle

Machine sewing, hand sewing and embroidery.

MACHINE OVERCASTING

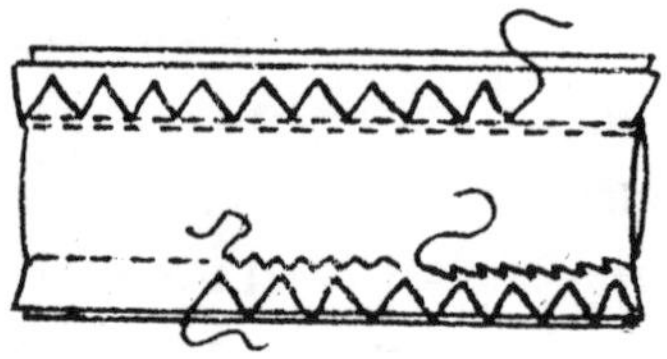

HAND OVERCASTING

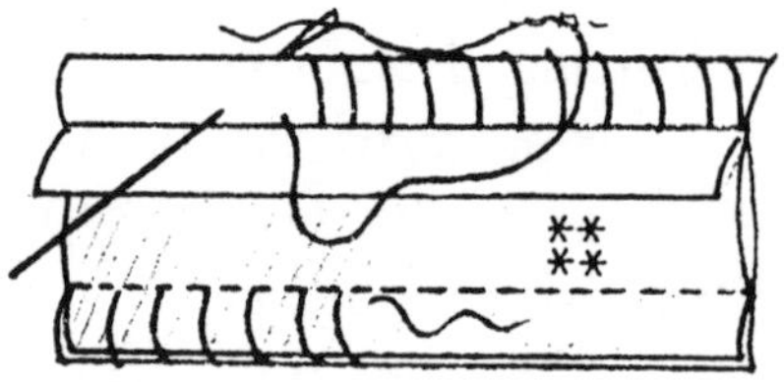

STEM/OUTLINE STITCH

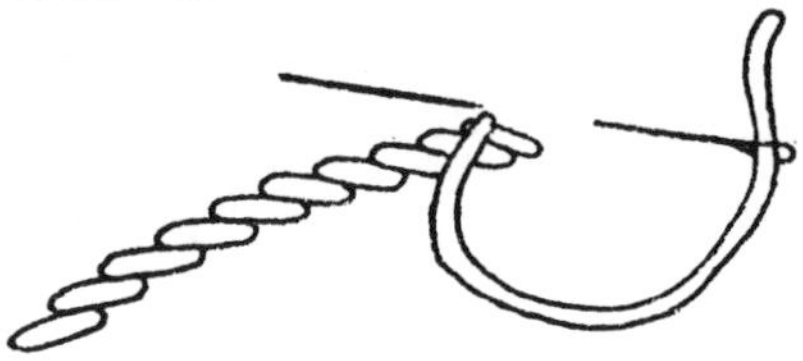

BACKSTITCH

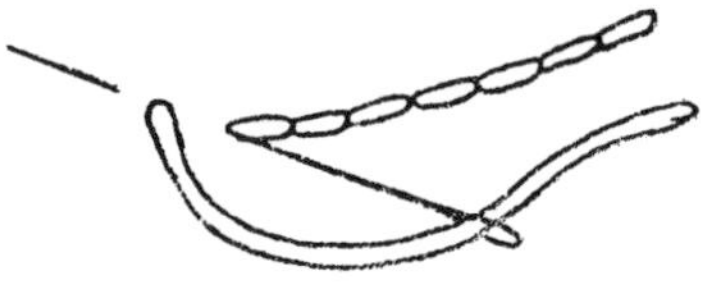

WHIP STITCH

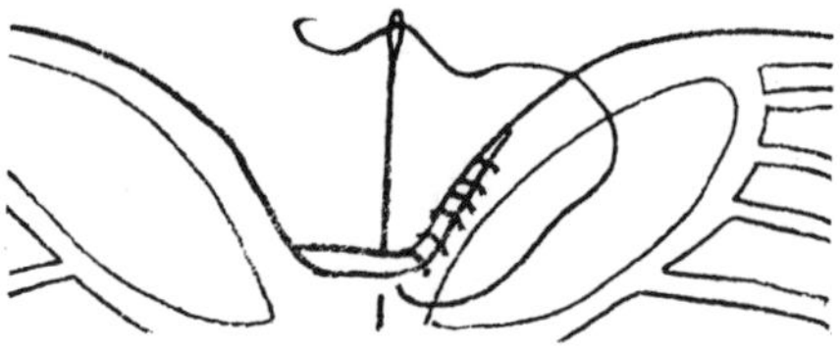

STRAIGHT STITCH

SATIN STITCH

LADDER STITCH

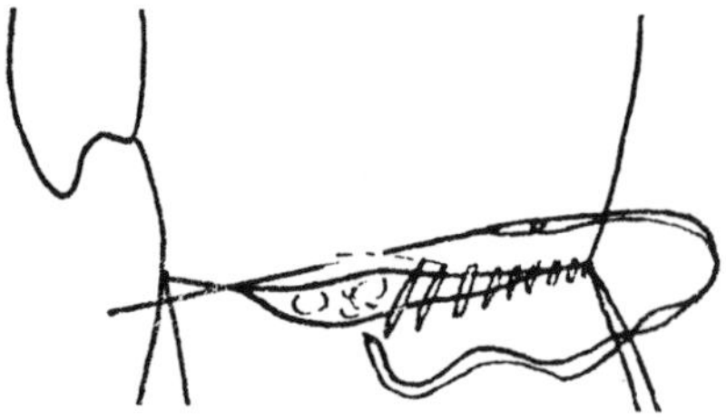

HINTS

Please read through the following information before starting to make your toy.

General toymaking equipment and requirements

Note: Specific items are listed in the requirements for each toy.

- *1 pair of scissors for cutting fabric only, (they don't have to be expensive) and 1 pair for paper and other materials*
- *A pen and sharp pencil*
- *Tape measure and ruler*
- *Semi-transparent paper or interfacing (woven), on which to trace patterns*
- *Tailor's chalk pencil, cloth marker pencil, transfer pencil and tracing paper or dressmaker's carbon paper and tracing wheel*
- *Sewing thread (polyester-covered cotton, if possible)*
- *Pins, machine and hand-sewing needles and unpicker/stitch ripper.*
- *A strong, thin, blunt object for use when stuffing*
- *Nail polish, clear*
- *Strong thread for sewing openings closed and attaching 'joggle' eyes*
- *Fabric glue (a quick-drying 'tacky' one, if possible)*

Tracing the pattern pieces onto paper

Using a sharp pencil, carefully trace the required pattern pieces onto semi-transparent white paper, such as lightweight typing paper or lined writing paper. (If the pattern pieces are to be used regularly, use interfacing instead of paper.) Record all the relevant information on the paper pattern such as the **name, number** and **(letter)** of each piece, the toys for which it is suitable (abbreviate, if necessary) and the straight grain arrow. Add any design lines, stripes or markings, where shown in the pattern sections.

For paper patterns which require a reversed pattern piece, such as those which are to be cut from a single layer of fabric or are to be painted (eg Tiger), place the paper pattern up against a window so that the light shines through. Trace all the markings onto the reverse side of the paper. Store pattern pieces in a plastic container or large envelope.

The selection and cutting of fabric

The toys in this book require a variety of different types of fabric, all with special characteristics. For example, the Birds and Butterflies require small amounts of a large range of colours; therefore, start a collection of dressmaking fabric. If a specific print or colour of fabric is needed, a piece 20 cm (8") wide of 90 cm (36") or 112 cm (45") wide fabric is enough for several toys.

Cotton fabrics are the easiest to work with, but any light- to medium-weight dressmaking fabric is suitable if you work with care. Fabrics with different textures or surface qualities can be used together, with interesting results. For example, when making a Bird, a taffeta or satin fabric could be used for the body and a more coarsely woven fabric, such as calico, used for the beak.

To assist in accurate cutting, the fabric should be ironed first if it is wrinkled or creased. This may seem a waste of time, but if you compare a fabric pattern piece cut from ironed fabric with a piece cut from wrinkled fabric which is later ironed, the difference in shape can be amazing.

Make sure when pinning the paper patterns on the fabrics that the arrow follows the straight grain. The straight grain runs parallel to the selvedge — the edge that has been finished to prevent fraying. Some fabrics have a distinct crossways grain also, so to take advantage of a particular 'print' the pattern pieces sometimes can be turned at right angles to the selvedge. The arrows should all follow the crossways grain. Remember, some shiny fabrics change colour when turned around, so have all the arrows pointing in the same direction.

Fleecy (tracksuit) fabric should not be mixed with dressmaking fabric, but can be used with fake fur fabric. Cut the pattern pieces from single or double thicknesses of fabric. Except for the Birds and painted Big Cats, either the inside (fleecy side) or the outside can be used as the right side. Paint only on the non-fleecy outside.

When cutting velvet or plush pile fabrics, do not attempt to cut from a double thickness of fabric because the pile will cause the fabric to move, even if it appears to be securely pinned.

Fake fur fabric has either a knitted or woven backing and the fur 'strokes' evenly in one direction only. Place the fabric fur side down on a table with the fur stroking towards you. When pinning the paper pattern pieces, the arrows should point towards you following the grain. If the fur, as well as the backing, have been cut on the edge closest to you, move them further away in order to take advantage of the length of the pile. When cutting the fabric, snip only through the backing, not the fur. Carefully pluck any loose bits of fur from the edges of the fabric shapes so that they won't get caught in your sewing machine.

Transferring markings onto fabric

Reference marks and design details can be transferred onto the fabric using a variety of methods. To find the most suitable method, experiment on a scrap of the fabric to be used first.

For thin, light-coloured fabrics, such as calico, place the fabric on top of the paper pattern and hold the pieces up *against a window* so that the light shines through. Carefully trace the design onto the fabric using a sharp *pencil* (eg a 2B) or a *cloth marker*. Cloth marker pencils sharpen to a very fine point and can be used for patchwork, fine embroidery and heirloom sewing. A sharp tailor's chalk pencil can be used but does not give a very fine line for delicate details such as those on the Butterfly Wings.

Iron-on transfer pencils are useful when transferring a design on thick or stretchy fabric, such as tracksuit (fleecy) fabric, prior to painting. Test first on a scrap of the fabric to be used because some light-coloured paints will allow the transferred line to show through.

With an ordinary pencil, trace the outline of the shape onto *tracing* paper or vegetable parchment *transfer paper*. Trace the design, using the transfer pencil. Position the transfer paper, drawn side down, on the fabric using the pencil line as a guide. Following the manufacturer's instructions iron the design onto the fabric. For a reversed fabric pattern piece, retrace the lines on the reverse side of the transfer paper and repeat the process.

For straight lines and bold designs, use *dressmaker's carbon paper* and a *tracing wheel*. For more intricate designs, place the dressmaker's carbon paper (not ordinary carbon paper — the ink mark will be permanent), coloured side up on a firm, flat surface. Put the fabric piece on top, with the side to be marked downwards.

Over this, position the paper or interfacing pattern (the paper tends to rip), with the drawn design upwards. Pressing firmly, trace over the design with an empty ballpoint pen. If necessary, make the lines clearer using a cloth marker.

Machine appliqué

Note: the following explanation deals specifically with the appliquéd Butterflies. Some of the methods may not be applicable to other projects.

For a toy Butterfly, cut two Wing shapes from fabric and two from Vilene/interfacing. Using the pen and carbon paper method or transfer pencil and tracing paper method, transfer the design onto the right side of each fabric wing. Tack the interfacing to the wrong side of each wing. Using the carbon paper or window method (for light colours), transfer the shape outlines onto the required scraps of coloured fabric. Cut out the shapes using the drawn or transferred lines. *Do not add seam allowances.* (For very small shapes, trace pairs or rows of shapes — cut around the group.) Put a small dab of fabric glue in the centre of each shape (wrong side) and stick in position on the fabric wing. (Test to see if a mark is made when the glue dries.) When the glue is dry, carefully snip away any excess fabric such as that between the shapes.

Select a close, wide zig zag or satin stitch. (Experiment to find the correct tension.) Stitch so that the outside edge of the satin stitch just covers the edge of the shape. To negotiate corners and curves, stitch, stopping with the needle in the fabric, lift the presser foot, turn the fabric and continue sewing so that the stitches overlap. To neaten the work, draw the upper threads to the wrong side, tie them and cut them off. When all the appliqué work is complete, add the satin stitch veins.

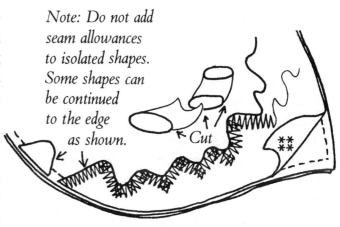

Note: Do not add seam allowances to isolated shapes. Some shapes can be continued to the edge as shown.

← Cut

Embroidered details

Other than the embroidery used instead of sewn on 'joggle' eyes or 'safety' eyes or noses, all the embroidery must be completed *before* stitching the toy together. When hand embroidery is to be worked on thin or lightweight fabric, (Butterfly or Bird wings) follow the same procedure as the appliqué Butterfly wings; ie transfer the design and attach the interfacing/Vilene. (Iron-on-Vilene can be used but the glue may give the fabric an undesired textural effect.) Embroider the design, using satin stitch or any other stitches of your choice. (Refer to the Glossary of Stitches.)

Painting with fabric paints

A very large range of fabric paints is commercially available. Some are permanent as soon as they are dry and others need ironing to fix the colours. They come in small tubs which require you to be able to paint neatly with a brush, or in easy-to-use squeeze bottles. The bottles range in size, starting at 30 ml (1 fl oz) and have different surface qualities. Choose a shiny or iridescent paint.

Transfer the design using one of the methods described, then paint using the desired colours. Ignore the manufacturer's directions to pre-wash the fabric if making a toy, because it will not require regular laundering. Paint the outline, then the area inside if painting a large shape. Always paint the shapes furthest away from you first so that your hand will not smudge a previously painted section. When using the squeeze bottles, do not attempt to do too much at one time or your hand will tire. Leave the fabric to dry flat.

Stitching methods and techniques for finishing raw edges

Just as different fabrics require different cutting methods, they also require different stitching methods.

Fleecy (tracksuit) fabric: sew, using a ballpoint or stretch sewing needle. Select a stretch sewing stitch such as a small zig zag. If you only have straight stitch, sew all the seams twice.

Velvet: This frays very easily when cut. Using straight stitch, sew once, then again 2 mm (1/16") away, within the seam allowance. After you sew each seam, clip the curves and whip stitch the edges of the fabric. Alternatively, if your machine has the capability, zig zag *over* the edge (overcast) or as close as possible to the edge without the fabric jamming in the feed dogs or needle plate. As you sew, carefully open out any concave curves and sew as if the edge were straight. The clips in the seam allowance will make this possible.

Warning — be prepared for lots of tiny fibres to cover you, your machine and the floor. Have a dust pan and brush or vacuum cleaner nearby. To tidy up the finished toy use a brush made for removing lint from clothing.

Despite the disadvantages involved in sewing with a luxurious fabric such as velvet, the elegant appearance of the finished toy is worth the effort.

Fur fabric: sew following the same method as for fleecy (tracksuit) fabric except when used in combination with velvet. The edges of woven fur, unlike the knitted variety of fur fabric, need to be overcast with zig zag stitch or whip stitched by hand — the fabric tends to weaken where stitched. Always tuck fur in, away from the raw edges when sewing.

Dressmaking fabric: the raw edges do not need to be finished, except for where shown in Bird instructions.

The importance of tying off threads

Not only can the tying off of threads save you time by making sure that the stitching of small seams does not come undone, it can also be used to your advantage in other ways.

For example, when joining the two sides of a Bird head together, a pin can be placed in the beaks and the threads from one end of the beak seam-tied to the corresponding threads on the other side of the head. Repeat for the other end of the beak seam and cut the threads off close to the (double) knot. The seams will now match accurately and there is less chance of the fabric slipping when the head is stitched. (Stuff a tulle butterfly with the cut off threads.)

If you are in the habit of backstitching (using the reverse button on your machine) at the beginning and end of *every* seam *every* time, then there is no need to tie off threads. If you are like me and tend to forget, it is easier to tie them when the seam is completed.

Seam-matching techniques

All the patterns in this book are full size and require *no enlargement*. If you trace your pattern pieces and cut your fabric accurately and use the correct seam allowance, the seams which are intended to match should match.

To test your seam widths, pin two pieces of fabric together, raw edges even. sew a seam with a 5 mm (¼″), or 8 mm (⅓″) seam allowance. Measure from the line of stitching to the raw edges of the fabric, to check that the distance is correct. If you have no guide marks on the needle plate or presser foot, you will need to stick a piece of masking tape to the needle plate. To establish the correct distance, mark the fabric at the required distance from the edge, stitch a few stitches and remove it from the machine. Check the distance with a ruler and, if it is correct, put the fabric back under the presser foot with the needle through one of the stitch holes in the fabric. Butt a piece of tape up against the raw edge making sure it does not cover the feed dogs.

Most seams can be matched using the thread-tying method. A problem arises when the angle of the seams at the raw edges of two panels to be joined, point in completely different directions. This happens when joining the Chest and Body Side seams of the female King parrot. For this type of situation, the seams 'match' or cross at a point along the length of the seam equal to the seam allowance being used. *Do not* try to make the seams match at the raw edges because when the seam is opened out they will not line up.

Turning the toy right side out and stuffing

Always take care when turning any part of the toy right side out. Check all the seams, make sure all the threads are securely knotted (double knot) and cut off close to the knot. Check that the curves and corners have been clipped and the raw edges overcast, if necessary.

Turn the toy using a blunt tool (eg a strong, thin knitting needle, wooden skewer or wooden end of a small paint brush), to push small pointed areas all the way out (eg wing tips). Do not push too hard or the seam may pop or fabric weaken into a hole.

Use the same blunt tool to push small amounts of stuffing into the extremities of the toy. Always stuff the areas furthest away from the opening first, then the rest of the toy, using progressively larger pieces of stuffing until the toy is stuffed firmly. Follow this procedure for each toy, unless directed otherwise in the basic directions.

Bags of toy stuffing are available in 200 g (7 oz), 500 g (17 oz) and 1 kg (2.2 lb) sizes. Only use polyester fibre fill; it is non-allergenic and machine washable.

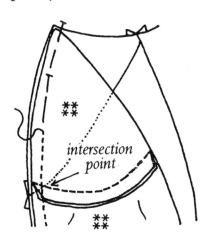

intersection point

**⁑ indicates wrong side of fabric

BUTTERFLIES

These 10 Australian butterflies, all quite different, are but a few of the myriad beautiful ones found in the world.

An accurate, true-to-life, representation can be made, or the designs simplified and stylised. Simply select the appropriate wing shape and add as many or as few decorative features as you desire.

The butterflies (common and scientific names) are as follows: Dingy Swallowtail (*Papilio anactus*), Blue Triangle (*Graphium sarpedon*), Evening Brown (*Melanitis leda*), Orchard (*Papilio aegeus*), Wanderer (*Danaus plexippus*), Blue-banded Eggfly (*Hypolimnas alimena*), Swordgrass Brown (*Tisiphone abeona*), Caper White (*Anaphaeis java*), Australian Admiral (*Pyrameis itea*) and the Lemon Migrant (*Catopsilia pomona*).

The toy butterflies measure approximately 25 cm (10″) across from wing tip to wing tip. The butterflies have antennae and 'joggle' eyes. Embroider the eyes if the toy is intended for a very young child.

The butterfly bodies can be made of fur fabric or any light- to medium-weight dressmaking fabric. On the underside, or belly, is a 'finger pocket' made by stitching a piece of elastic to the body. Slip a finger into the pocket and move your hand up and down to make the wings flap. (Because they can be made to move these toys are referred to as 'finger-action' toys.) Colours and pattern details can be added using one of three methods: machine appliqué, fabric painting or embroidery.

Before starting to make your toy, please read carefully through the section on Hints (see page 3), for information on the following subjects:

- General toymaking equipment and requirements.
- Tracing the pattern pieces onto paper.
- The selection and cutting of fabric.
- Transferring the markings onto fabric.
- Machine appliqué.
- Embroidered details.
- Painting with fabric paints.
- Turning the toy right side out and stuffing.

MATERIALS FOR EACH BUTTERFLY

- *1 pair of 8 mm (⅓″) or 10 mm (⅜″) 'joggle' sew-on eyes (black, red or blue centres)*
- *Embroidery floss (instead of eyes — on young child's toy)*
- *1 x 12 cm (4¾″) length of hat elastic, leather thonging or flat elastic*
- *1 piece 4 cm wide or 2 pieces 2 cm wide elastic, 4 cm (1½″) long*
- *1 piece fabric for the wings, 30 cm x 30 cm (12″ x 12″)*
- *1 piece fabric for the body, 10 cm x 15 cm (4″ x 6″)*
- *Polyester fibre filling (200 g [7 oz] is sufficient for many toys)*

BUTTERFLY PATTERN SECTION

For toy: cut 2 Wing shapes from fabric and 2 Body shapes from fabric

arrow indicates straight grain of fabric and stroke of fur

seam allowance 5 mm (¼'')

To make a paper pattern:
Trace wing on to paper; fold and transfer all details up against a window; cut out

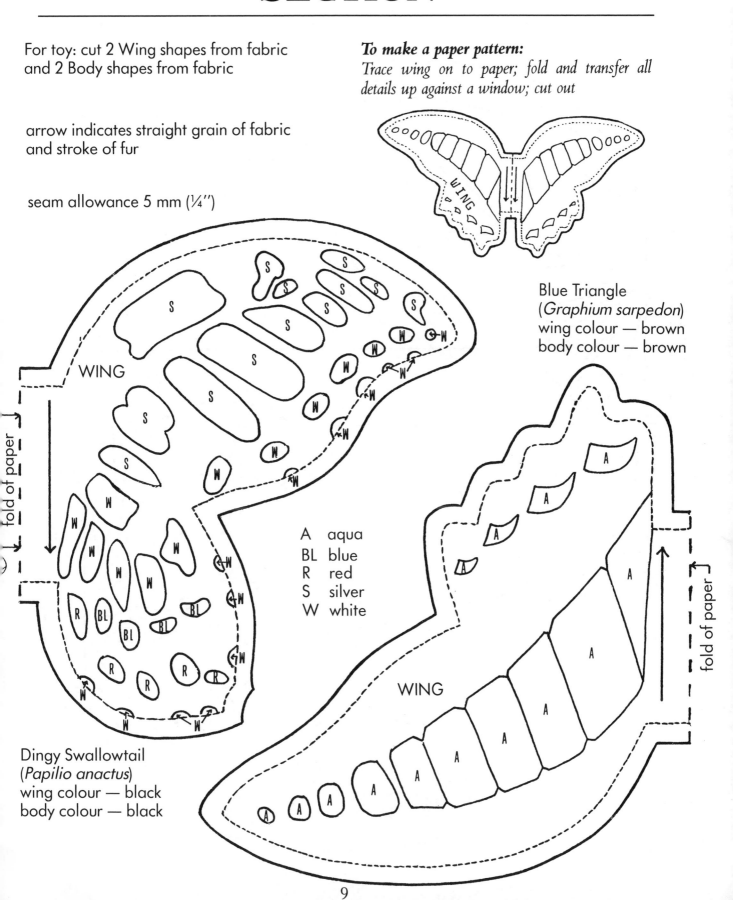

Blue Triangle
(*Graphium sarpedon*)
wing colour — brown
body colour — brown

A   aqua
BL   blue
R   red
S   silver
W   white

WING

fold of paper

Dingy Swallowtail
(*Papilio anactus*)
wing colour — black
body colour — black

WING

fold of paper

arrow indicates straight grain of fabric

For toy: cut 2 Wing shapes and 2 Body shapes from fabric

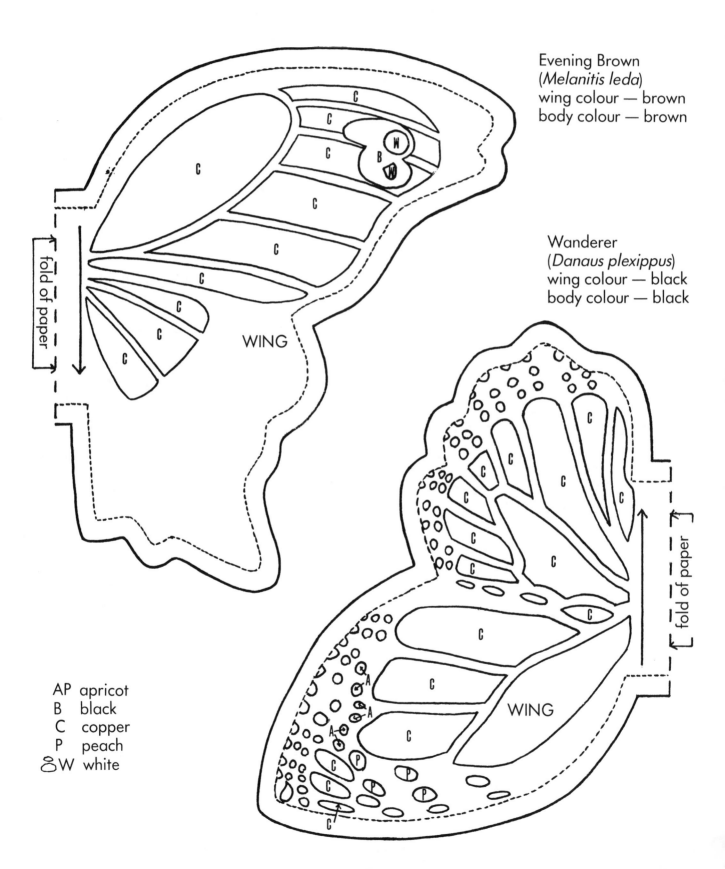

Evening Brown
(*Melanitis leda*)
wing colour — brown
body colour — brown

Wanderer
(*Danaus plexippus*)
wing colour — black
body colour — black

AP   apricot
B   black
C   copper
P   peach
⊗W white

appliqué the wings, then satin stitch the veins in black

seam allowance 5 mm (¼'')

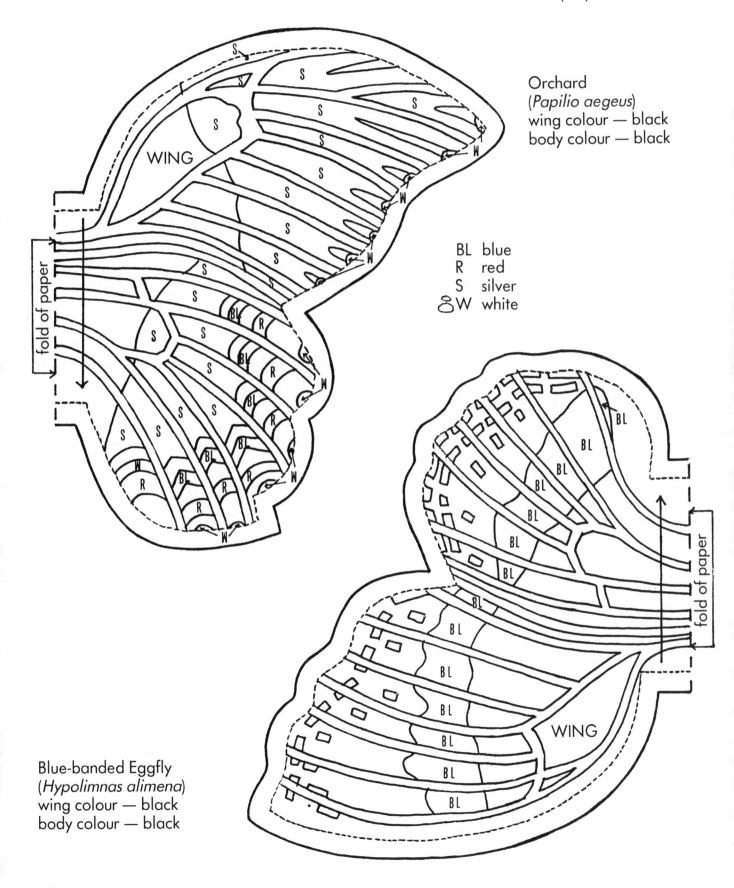

Orchard
(*Papilio aegeus*)
wing colour — black
body colour — black

BL blue
R   red
S   silver
&W white

WING

fold of paper

Blue-banded Eggfly
(*Hypolimnas alimena*)
wing colour — black
body colour — black

WING

fold of paper

arrow indicates straight grain of fabric
and stroke of fur

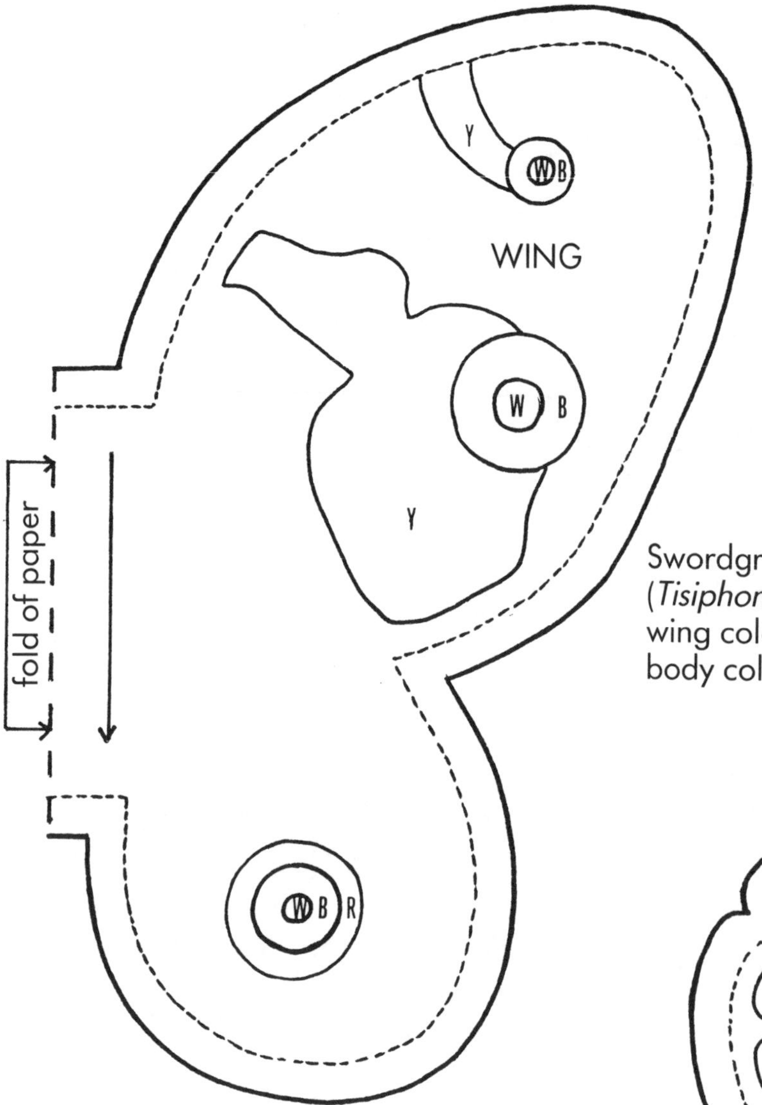

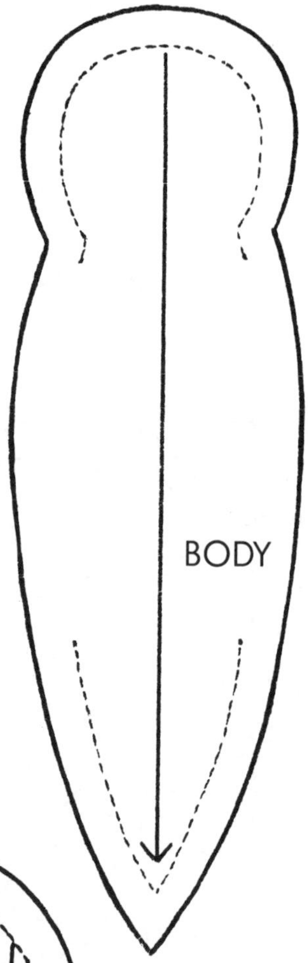

WING

fold of paper

Swordgrass Brown
(*Tisiphone abeona*)
wing colour — brown
body colour — brown

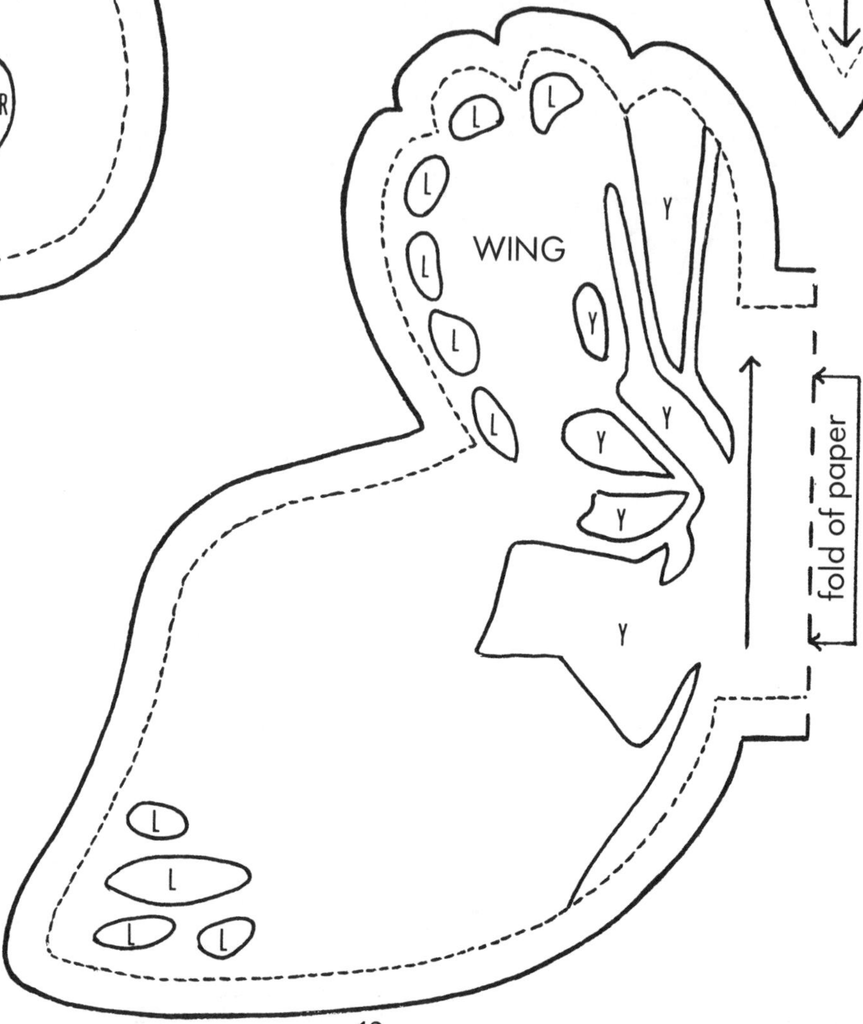

BODY

WING

fold of paper

B   black
L   lemon
R   red
W   white
Y   yellow

Caper White
(*Anaphaeis java*)
underwing design
wing colour — brown
body colour — yellow

12

For toy: Cut 2 Wing shapes and 2 Body shapes from fabric

seam allowance 5 mm (¼")

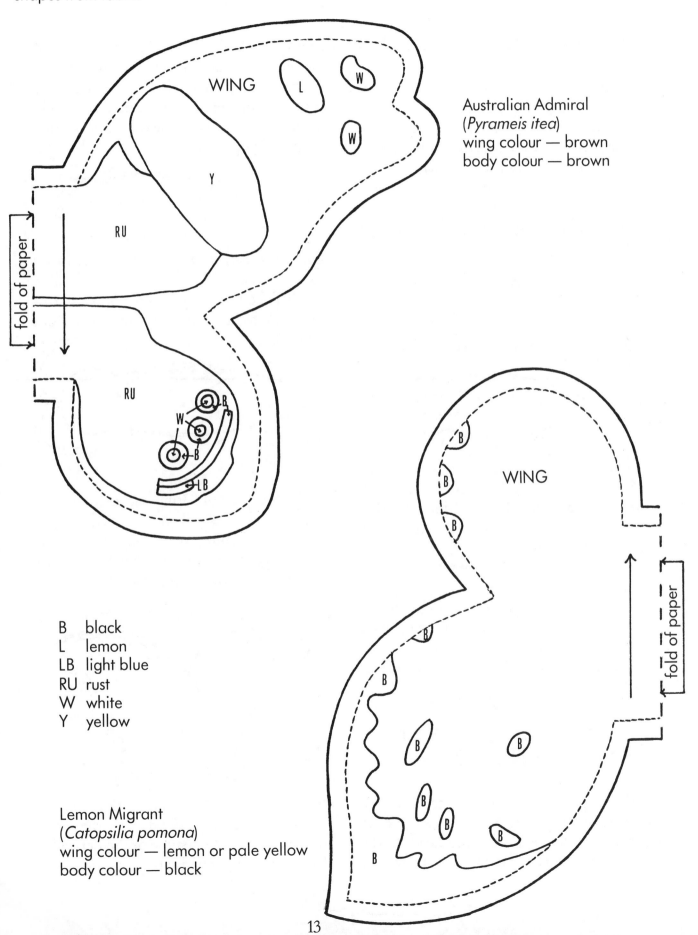

WING

Australian Admiral
(*Pyrameis itea*)
wing colour — brown
body colour — brown

fold of paper

RU

Y

RU

W

B

B

LB

B   black
L   lemon
LB light blue
RU rust
W   white
Y   yellow

WING

fold of paper

Lemon Migrant
(*Catopsilia pomona*)
wing colour — lemon or pale yellow
body colour — black

13

BUTTERFLY INSTRUCTIONS

METHOD FOR BUTTERFLIES

Ten different butterflies can be made from the one set of pattern pieces.
- *Follow the designs provided to decorate the wings with machine appliqué, fabric paint or hand embroidery (before you start to sew), or cut the wings from plain or printed fabric.*
- *The illustrations which accompany these directions show the Evening Brown butterfly wing shape.*

Body

1. Tack a 12 cm (4¾″) length of hat elastic, leather thonging or 4 mm (¼″) wide flat elastic to the centre of the head of one Body (Fig. 1).

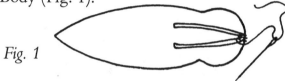

Fig. 1

2. Cut a 4 cm (1½″) length of 4 cm (1½″) wide elastic or two lengths of 2 cm (¾″) wide elastic. (Butt the long sides together and join with zig zag stitching or by hand.) Or, cut a 4 cm (1½″) wide length of 7.5 cm (3″) wide elastic lengthways. (Overcast the cut edges to stop fraying.) Pin the elastic to the other Body piece. Stitch close to the edge from one lower edge of the elastic, across the neck to the other lower edge (Fig. 2). This forms the finger pocket.

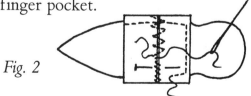

Fig. 2

3. Having the antennae enclosed, pin the body pieces together. Sew from the elastic at the neck edge around the head to the other neck edge, 5 mm (¼″) from the edges. Stitch also from the lower edge of the elastic to the tail tip and finish at the elastic on the other side (Fig. 3). Trim the edges of the elastic to match the body shape and turn, right side out, through one of the side openings.

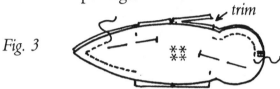

Fig. 3

Tuck fur in away from raw edges when sewing

4. Stuff the head of the body. Stitch across the neck to stop the stuffing coming out (Fig. 4).

Fig. 4

Wings

1. Pin the pair of Wing pieces together. Stitch 5 mm (¼″) from the raw edges, leaving an opening for turning at the neck edge (Fig. 1). Clip the curves and turn right side out, one wing at a time.

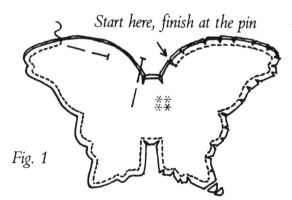

Start here, finish at the pin

Fig. 1

Note: The decorated wings will be harder to turn right side out, due to the extra thickness of the paint or interfacing/ Vilene and appliquéd fabric shapes.

2. Starting with the wing tip furthest from the neck opening, stuff the wing so that it is flat and not bulky. *Do not stuff* the body position, instead, pin from the neck to the tail edge. Stuff the other side of the wing, pinning in the same manner. Hand whip stitch or ladder stitch the neck opening closed (Fig. 2). Stitch down both sides of the body position to keep the stuffing in place.

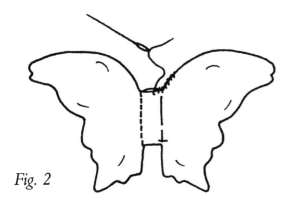

Fig. 2

Completing the toy
1. Folding the stuffed wing piece a little, thread the wing through the side openings of the body until the body is in the centre (Fig. 1). Stuff the upperside of the body, including the tail. (The upperside is the one without the elastic.) Turn under the 5 mm (¼″) seam allowances and sew by hand. Attach the body to the wing piece, using the previous row of stitching as a guide. Turn over and around, repeating the procedure for all the side seams of the body. (Do not stuff the underside of the body.)

Three different ways of decorating the toy are shown in the illustration. The Butterfly can also be left plain.

Note: The embroidered eyes can be a circle of black satin stitch or white satin stitch, with a black pupil.

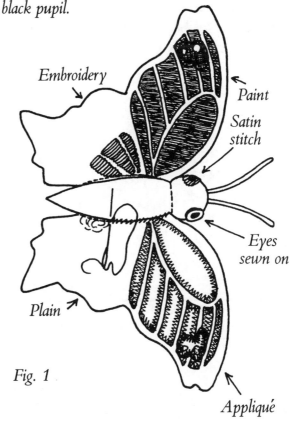

Embroidery

Paint

Satin stitch

Eyes sewn on

Plain

Fig. 1

Appliqué

Note: Make sure that the elastic is tucked into the seam. If using fur fabric, sew through the backing also, not just the fur.

2. Sew 'joggle' eyes in position on the side of the head, or embroider using satin stitch (Fig. 1).

3. Paint the end of the hat elastic with clear nail polish, or tie a knot to stop the end fraying and looking untidy.

BUTTERFLY BABY QUILT

Finished size 85 cm x 55 cm (33½″ x 21½″). Use plain and appliquéd butterflies, *or* painted *or* embroidered ones. (The methods described may not be suitable for larger-sized quilts.)

Method

1. For each Butterfly, cut one Body piece from fabric, one from Vilene. (Non-woven stiffener.) Follow step 3 of the butterfly **body** directions; ignore references to antennae and finger pocket elastic. Start sewing tail tip 4 cm (1½″) from the neck and finish in a corresponding position.

2. Cut one Wing shape from fabric, (decorate as described in the Hints section, see page 3) and one from Vilene. Sew, following step 1 of the **wing** directions.

3. With the fabric sides facing upwards, thread the wings through the body so that the body is in the centre. Turn under the seam allowances, pin and iron also, if you wish.

4. Make a full-sized paper pattern of your quilt, including quilting lines and butterfly positions. Cut two rectangles of fabric the

desired size. (Use fleecy tracksuit fabric as it has 'give'.) Using a tracing wheel and dressmaker's carbon paper, transfer the lines onto one piece of fabric. Pin the Butterflies in position. Stitching 2 mm (1⁄16″) from the edges, sew in place, starting with the body shape, followed by the wings.

5. Draw all the threads to the wrong side, tie and cut off. Place the other piece of fabric on top, right sides facing. Pin these pieces on top of a sheet of wadding. Leaving an opening for turning, stitch 5 mm (¼″) from the edge. Clip the corners off.

6. Turn right side out and hand sew the opening closed. Topstitch 5 mm (¼″) from the outer edge, using a long stitch.

7. With long hand-tacking stitches, sew from the centre of the quilt to each corner and the centre of each side. Try to avoid wrinkling the fabric.

8. Using a long machine stitch, sew on the background fabric 5 mm (¼″) away from the edge of each Butterfly shape. Stitch following the transferred quilting lines. Draw all the threads to the back, tie and cut off, close to the knot.

BIRDS

Australia is well known for its beautiful, brightly coloured parrots and cockatoos. With their realistic appearance, these toy birds will be instantly recognisable to most. There's the familar 'cocky', the Sulphur-crested white cockatoo and the Galah, both popular cage birds that can also be seen in large numbers in the bush.

Ten different birds can be made from this set of mix-and-match, multiple-choice pattern pieces. The types of bird included are the Gang Gang Cockatoo (male and female variations), the little white Corella, King Parrot (male and female), Galah, Sulphur-crested White Cockatoo (with crest up or down) and the Major Mitchell Pink Cockatoo (with crest up or down).

Each bird measures approximately 25 cm (10″) in length, except the white and pink cockatoos with their crests up. They measure 30 cm (12″) in length. Depending on the age of the child for whom the toy is intended, choose either 'joggle' eyes or embroider the eyes in satin stitch. Loops of elastic form the feet or claws and enable the bird to 'perch' on your finger. Push your finger through both loops of elastic and move your hand up and down to make the bird's wings flap and the tail move. (I refer to these as 'finger-action' toys.) Details such as wing and tail feathers can be added using embroidery (outline-stem stitch) or fabric paint. Try to keep the toy simple in appearance — don't overdo the embellishment.

Made by sewing together patches or pieces of different coloured fabrics, the completed toy is, in a sense, a three-dimensional example of patchwork. Follow the realistic design and colours listed or make your own unique 'patchwork' bird. Use either plain or patterned fabrics such as 'cottage prints'. Use colours to match your decor, or those of a favourite sporting team, or your child's school colours. Mix-and-match the head, body, wing and tail panels of different birds, too, if you wish. Refer to the pattern section and the illustrations which accompany the preliminary joining procedure instructions. Notice how the individual pieces are joined to make a basic bird pattern shape.

Suitable fabrics include any light- to medium-weight dressmaking fabric such as cotton, polycotton, polyester, taffeta, satin or calico. Combine several types of fabric with different textures for an interesting effect. Fleecy (tracksuit) fabric can also be used. (Only use fleecy with fleecy.)

Before starting to make your toy please read carefully through the section on Hints (page 3), for information on the following subjects:
- General toymaking equipment and requirements
- Tracing the pattern pieces onto paper
- The selection and cutting of fabric
- The importance of tying off threads
- Seam-matching techniques
- Painting with fabric paints
- Embroidered details
- Turning the toy right side out and stuffing

MATERIALS FOR EACH BIRD

- *1 pair of 8 mm (⅓″) or 10 mm (⅜″) 'joggle' eyes with black centres (or red for Galah)*
- *1 skein of black embroidery floss to embroider eyes on a young child's toy*
- *2 x 4 cm (1½″) lengths of 12 mm (½″) wide elastic, (two small elastic bands)*
- *Polyester fibre filling. 200 g (7 oz) is sufficient for a number of toys*
- *Fabric-A 20 cm (8″) length of 112 cm (45″) wide fabric is enough for two single-colour birds*
- *Small amounts of a variety of colours are also needed, check the lists for the colours required*

Note: Remember, only one of each paper pattern piece need be cut out. Mark the paper pattern with all the markings and the names of the birds for which it is suitable. (You may want to make a different bird in the future and this saves you having to trace the piece a second time.) When referring to the lists of pattern pieces, make a note of the **name**, **number** and **(letter)** given for each piece. This ensures that the correct piece is selected.

Gang Gang (female)
Beak cut 2 light grey
Head 1 cut 2 mottled grey
Chest cut 1 mottled grey
Centre Front cut 1 mottled grey
Lower Front cut 1 mottled grey
Back Gusset cut 1 mottled grey
Body Side cut 2 mottled grey
Wing cut 4 mottled grey
Tail 1 cut 2 mottled grey
Black elastic

Gang Gang (male)
Beak cut 2 light grey
Upperhead 1 cut 2 mottled grey
Lowerhead (A) cut 2 mottled grey
Lowerhead (B) cut 2 red

Lowerhead (C) cut 2 mottled grey
Chest cut 1 mottled grey
Centre Front cut 1 mottled grey
Lower Front cut 1 mottled grey
Back Gusset cut 1 mottled grey
Body Side cut 2 mottled grey
Wing cut 4 mottled grey
Tail 1 cut 2 mottled grey
Black elastic

Note: When the direction is given to cut two of a particular colour, this means that a pair of fabric pieces is needed. Thus, if you are cutting on a single thickness of fabric, turn the paper pattern over so that it is reversed (R). Keep the straight grain arrow pointing the same way as all the other pieces.

Corella (Little White Corella)
Beak cut 2 bone
Head 3 cut 2 white
Chest cut 1 white
Centre Front cut 1 white
Lower Front cut 1 white
Back Gusset cut 1 white
Body Side cut 2 white
Wing cut 2 white
Underwing (A) cut 2 white
Underwing (B) cut 2 sulphur/yellow
Underwing (C) cut 2 white
Tail 1 cut 1 white
Tail Front (A) cut 1 sulphur/yellow
Tail Front (B) cut 1 white
Black elastic

Of the Birds listed on this page the Gang Gang (female) is the easiest, requiring no preliminary joining. The Corella requires the most preliminary joining and is, therefore, a little more difficult.

King Parrot (female)
Beak cut 2 grey
Upperhead 2 cut 2 green

Lowerhead (D) cut 2 lime/light green
Lowerhead (E) cut 2 green
Chest (A) cut 1 lime/light green
Chest (B) cut 1 red/scarlet
Centre Front cut 1 red/scarlet
Lower Front cut 1 red/scarlet
Back Gusset (AB) cut 1 green
Back Gusset (C) cut 1 royal blue
Body Side (A) cut 2 lime/light green
Body Side (B) cut 2 red/scarlet
Body Side (C) cut 2 royal blue
Wing cut 4 green
Tail 2 cut 1 dark blue/blackish blue
Tail 2 cut 1 green (for tail back)
Black or white elastic

Galah
Beak cut 2 bone
Upperhead 3 cut 2 pale pink
Lowerhead cut 2 salmon pink
Chest cut 1 salmon pink
Centre Front cut 1 salmon pink
Lower Front cut 1 grey
Back gusset (A) cut 1 salmon pink
Back Gusset (BC) cut 1 grey
Body Side (AB) cut 2 salmon pink
Body Side (C) cut 2 grey
Wing cut 2 grey
Underwing (A) cut 2 salmon pink
Underwing (BC) cut 2 grey
Tail 1 cut 2 dark grey
White elastic

White (Sulphur-crested) Cockatoo
*With crest up or down
Beak cut 2 black
Head 2 cut 2 white
Crest Up cut 2 sulphur/yellow OR
Crest Down cut 2 sulphur/yellow
Chest cut 1 white
Centre Front cut 1 white
Lower Front cut 1 white
Back Gusset cut 1 white
Body Side cut 2 white
Wing cut 2 white

Underwing (A) cut 2 white
Underwing (B) cut 2 sulphur/yellow
Underwing (C) cut 2 white
Tail 1 cut 1 white
Tail Front (A) cut 1 sulphur/yellow
Tail Front (B) cut 1 white
Black elastic

King Parrot (male)
Beak cut 2 light red
Head 2 cut 2 red/scarlet
Chest cut 1 red/scarlet
Centre Front cut 1 red/scarlet
Lower Front cut 1 red/scarlet
Back Gusset (A) cut 1 royal blue
Back Gusset (B) cut 1 emerald green
Back Gusset (C) cut 1 royal blue
Body Side (AB) cut 2 red/scarlet
Body Side (C) cut 2 royal blue
Upperwing (A) cut 2 emerald green
Upperwing (B) cut 2 light green
Upperwing (C) cut 2 emerald green
Wing cut 2 emerald green
Tail 2 cut 2 dark blue/blackish blue
Black or white elastic

Pink (Major Mitchell) Cockatoo
*With crest up or down
Beak cut 2 bone
Upperhead 2(A) cut 2 white
Upperhead 2(B) cut 2 pink
Lowerhead cut 2 pink
Chest cut 1 pink
Centre Front cut 1 pink
Lower Front cut 1 white
Back Gusset (A) cut 1 pink
Back Gusset (BC) cut 1 white
Body Side (AB) cut 2 pink
Body Side (C) cut 2 white
Wing cut 2 white
Underwing (AB) cut 2 pink/peach
Underwing (C) cut 2 white
Tail 1 cut 1 white
Tail Front (A) cut 1 pink/peach
Tail Front (B) cut 1 white
Black elastic

Crest Up — paper pattern
(Join the fabric pieces first then use the Crest Up paper pattern for the final cutting.)
Crest Up (A) cut 2 white
Crest Up (B) cut 2 red
Crest Up (C) cut 2 yellow
Crest Up (D) cut 2 red
Crest Up (E) cut 1 white

OR

Crest Down — paper pattern
(Join the fabric pieces first then use the Crest Down paper pattern for the final cutting.)
Crest Down (A) cut 2 white
Crest Down (B) cut 2 red
Crest Down (C) cut 1 white

Of the Birds listed on the previous page the Galah is the easiest requiring some preliminary joining. The Pink (Major Mitchell) Cockatoo with its crest up is the most difficult of all the Birds. It is recommended that you try one of the easier birds before attempting it.

arrow indicates straight grain of fabric

seam allowance 5 mm (¼")

⊕ indicates position of eye

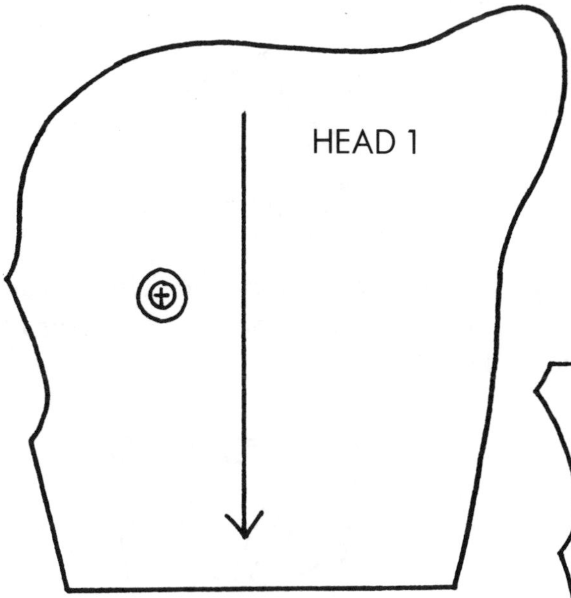

HEAD 1

⊕

suitable for Gang Gang (female)

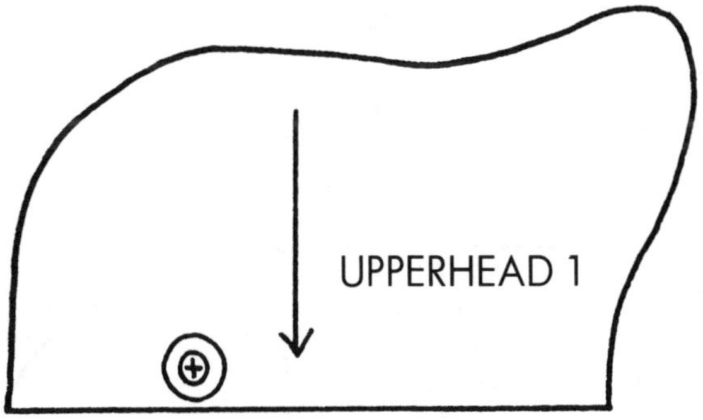

UPPERHEAD 1

⊕

suitable for Gang Gang (male)

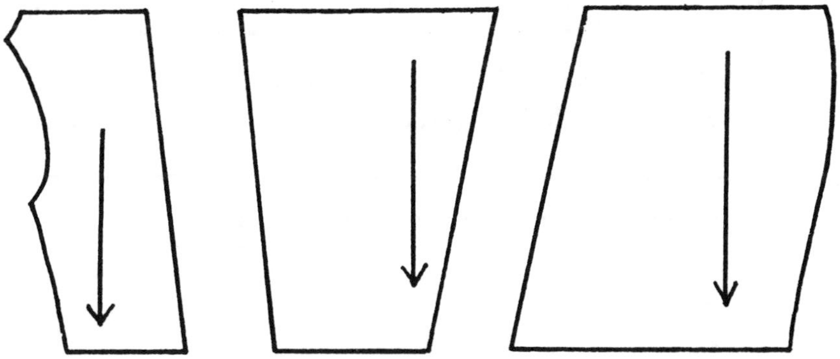

LOWERHEAD (A)   LOWERHEAD (B)   LOWERHEAD (C)

suitable for Gang Gang (male)

Preliminary Joining Procedure

Note: Work on both sides of the head at the same time following the same steps but reversing the pieces accordingly.

Step 1: Pin the Lowerhead (A) to the Lowerhead (B) piece (Fig. 1). Sew 5 mm (¼") from the edge.

Step 2: Pin and stitch the Lowerhead (C) piece to the other Lowerhead pieces (Fig. 2). Tie off all threads.

Step 3: Pin and sew the Upperhead 1 piece to the Lowerhead pieces (Fig. 3).

The male Gang Gang head pieces are now ready to continue as for the bird instructions.

✱✱ indicates wrong side of fabric

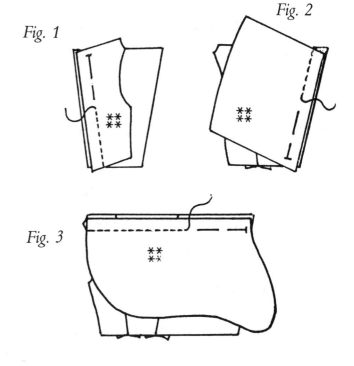

Fig. 1   *Fig. 2*

Fig. 3

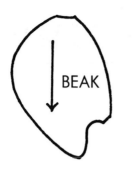

Beak suitable for all Birds

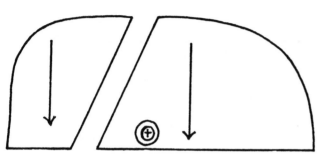

UPPERHEAD 2(A)   UPPERHEAD 2(B)
suitable for Pink Cockatoo

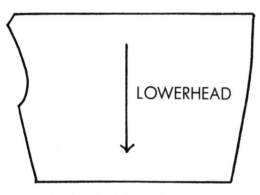

suitable for Galah and Pink Cockatoo

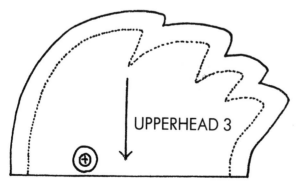

suitable for Galah

stitching guide indicated by dotted line

arrow indicates straight grain of fabric

Preliminary Joining Procedure

Step 1: Pin and sew an Upperhead 2(A) piece to each Upperhead 2(B) piece (Fig. 1).

Fig. 1

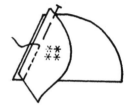

Step 2: Pin and stitch the Upperhead pieces to the corresponding Lowerhead piece (Fig. 2).

Fig. 2

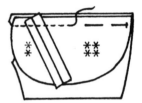

The Pink Cockatoo head pieces are now ready to continue as for the Bird instructions.

Preliminary Joining Procedure

Pin and stitch the Upperhead 3 piece to the Lowerhead piece, 5 mm (¼″) from the edge (Fig. 1). Repeat.

Fig. 1

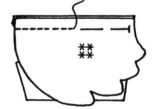

The Galah head pieces are now ready to continue as for the Bird instructions.

✷✷ indicates wrong side of fabric

⊕ indicates position of eye

seam allowance 5 mm (¼″)

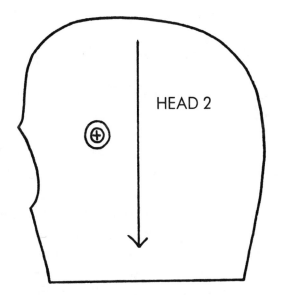

HEAD 2

suitable for King Parrot (male) and White Cockatoo

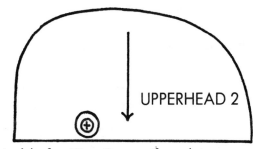

UPPERHEAD 2

suitable for King Parrot (female)

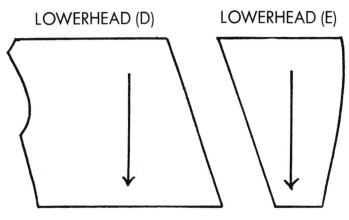

LOWERHEAD (D)

LOWERHEAD (E)

suitable for King Parrot (female)

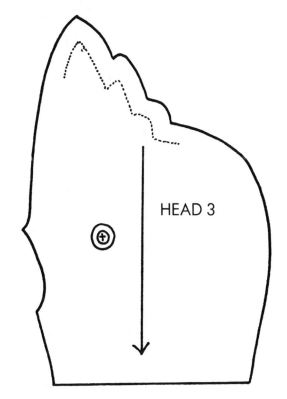

HEAD 3

suitable for Corella

Stitching guide for Corella head indicated by dotted line. Seam allowance 5 mm (¼″).

Preliminary Joining Procedure

Step 1: Pin and stitch a Lowerhead (E) piece to each Lowerhead (D) piece (Fig. 1).

Step 2: Pin and sew an Upperhead 2 piece to the corresponding Lowerhead pieces (Fig. 2).

Continue as for Bird instructions.

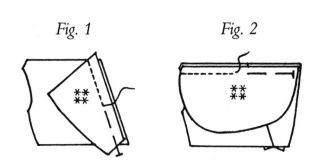

Fig. 1

Fig. 2

Marks on Centre Front, indicate position of elastic, used to form loops for Birds feet. See Bird instructions

ELASTIC GUIDE: 4 cm (1½") length of 6 mm (¼") wide elastic

Preliminary Joining Procedure

Step 1: Match the centre of the curved edges of the Chest (A) and Chest (B) pieces (Fig. 1).
Step 2: Pin and stitch the pieces together (Fig. 2).
The King Parrot (female) Chest is now ready to continue with the Bird instructions.

Note: Remember that when matching the seams of the Chest with the Body Side the seams match or cross 5 mm (¼") from the edge, along the length of the seam. Don't try to make the seams match at the raw edges because when the seam is opened out the seams will not line up.

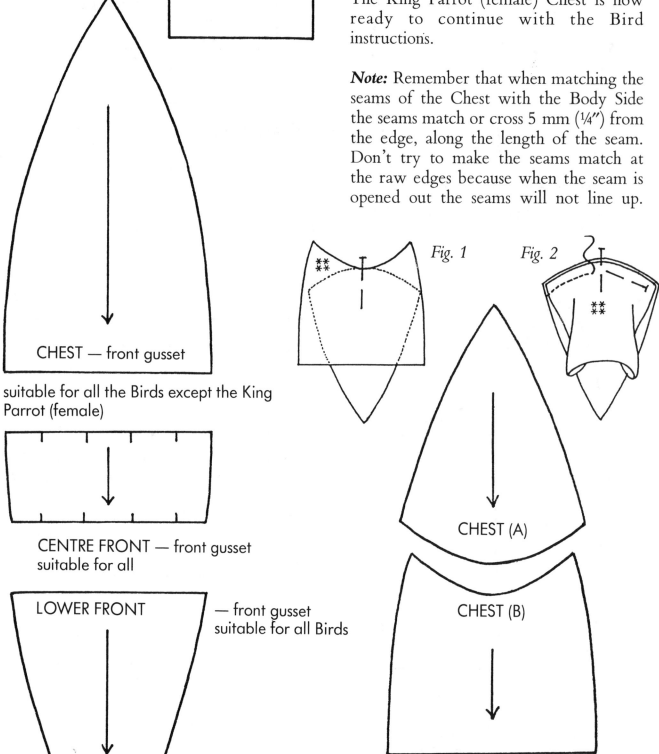

CHEST — front gusset

suitable for all the Birds except the King Parrot (female)

CENTRE FRONT — front gusset
suitable for all

LOWER FRONT — front gusset suitable for all Birds

Fig. 1   Fig. 2

CHEST (A)

CHEST (B)

suitable for King Parrot (F)

arrow indicates straight grain of fabric

seam allowance 5 mm (¼″)

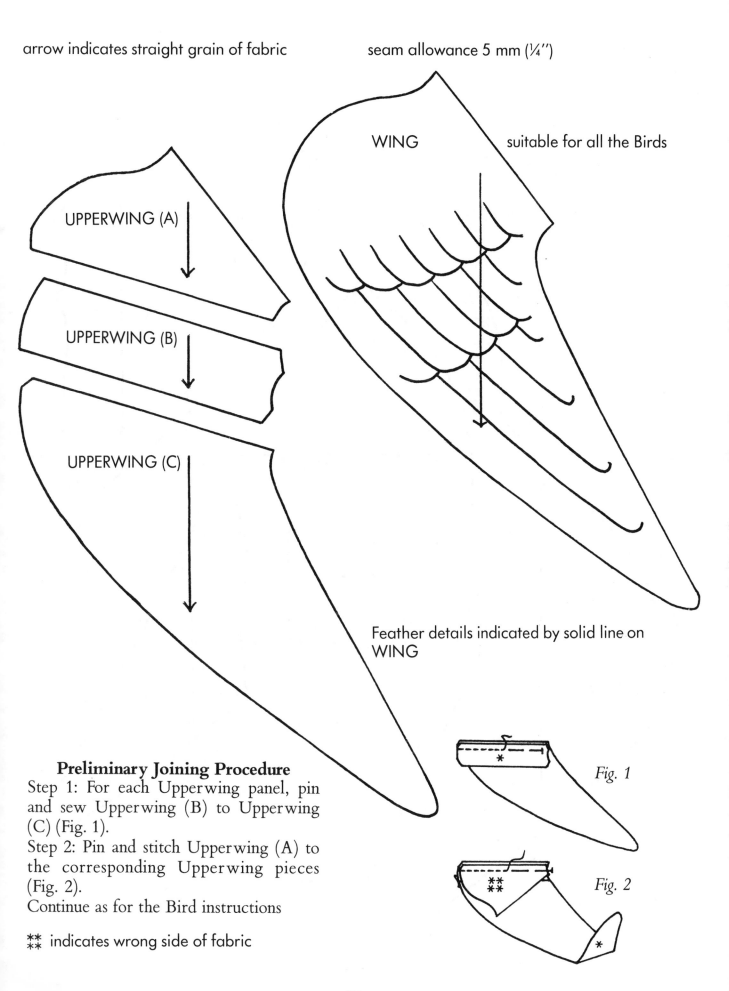

UPPERWING (A)

UPPERWING (B)

UPPERWING (C)

WING

suitable for all the Birds

Feather details indicated by solid line on WING

Fig. 1

Fig. 2

Preliminary Joining Procedure
Step 1: For each Upperwing panel, pin and sew Upperwing (B) to Upperwing (C) (Fig. 1).
Step 2: Pin and stitch Upperwing (A) to the corresponding Upperwing pieces (Fig. 2).
Continue as for the Bird instructions

** indicates wrong side of fabric

arrow indicates straight grain of fabric   seam allowance 5 mm (¼″)

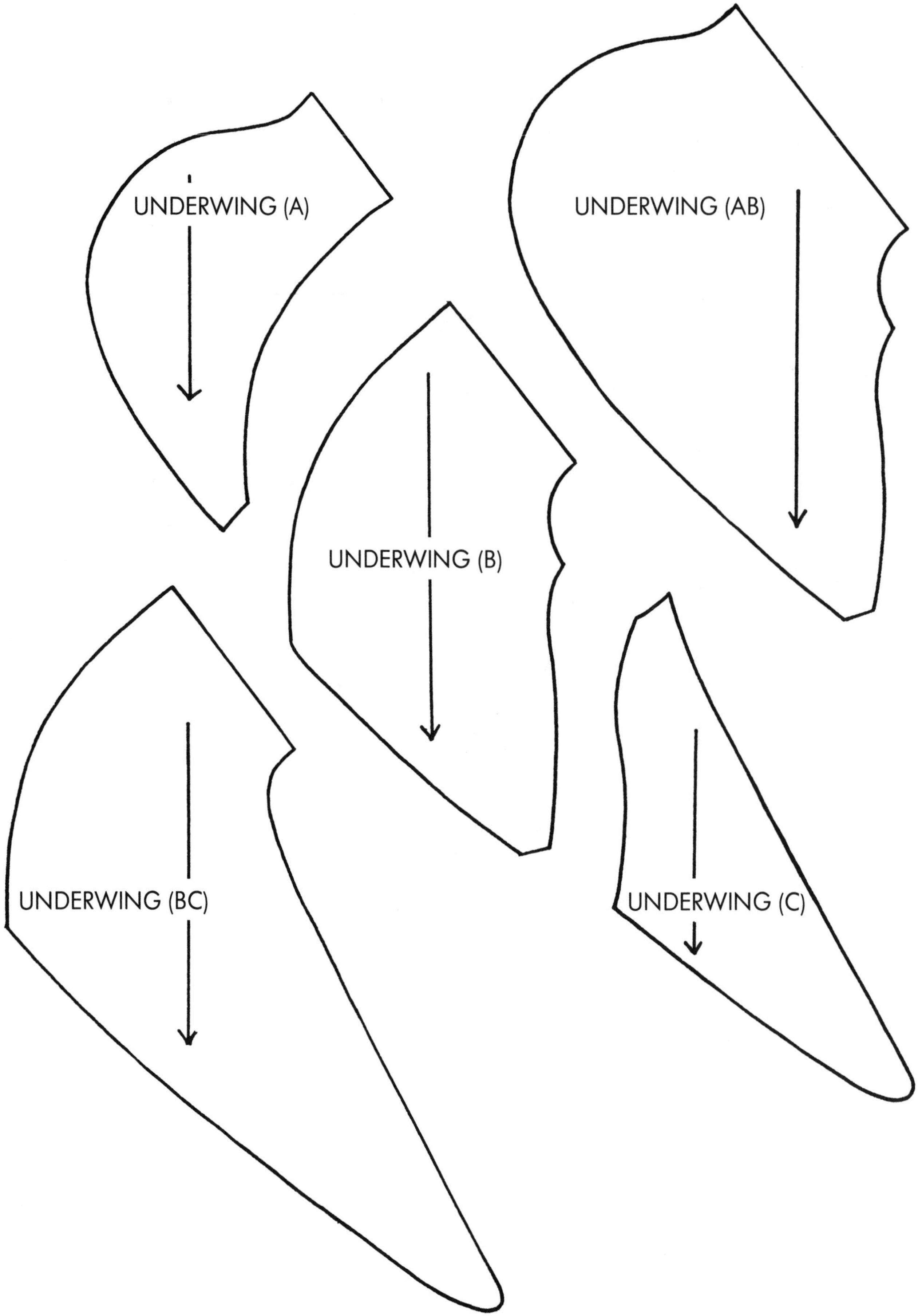

UNDERWING (A)

UNDERWING (AB)

UNDERWING (B)

UNDERWING (BC)

UNDERWING (C)

Preliminary Joining Procedure

Step 1: For each Underwing panel, pin and stitch Underwing (A) to Underwing (B) (Fig. 1).

Step 2: Pin and sew Underwing (C) to Underwing (A) and (B) or Underwing (AB) (Fig. 2).

Fig. 1

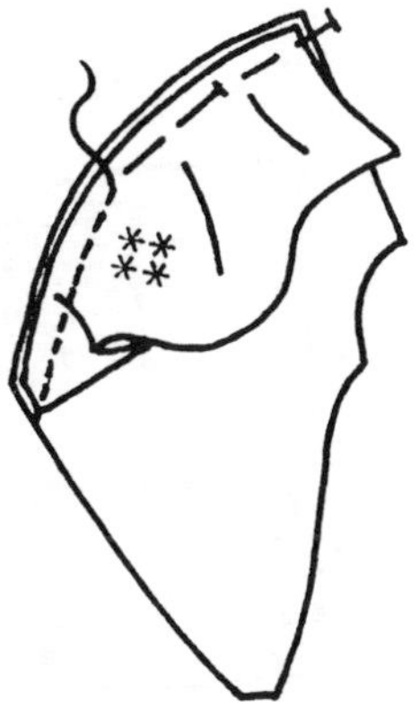

Fig. 2

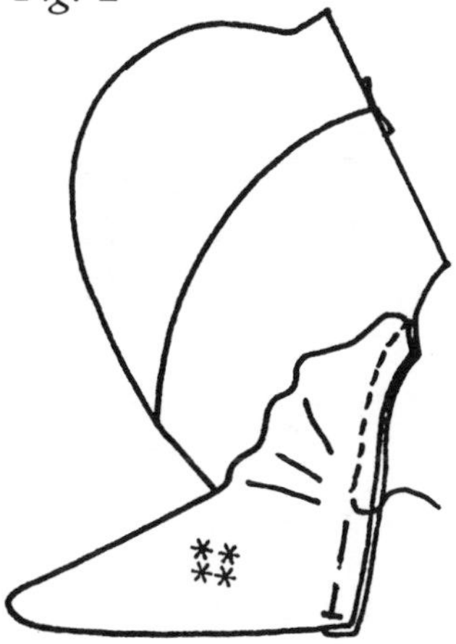

Note: The same method applies when joining Underwing (A) to Underwing (BC). The Underwing is now ready to continue as for Bird instructions.

** indicates wrong side of fabric

Underwing combinations include:
(A) + (B) + (C), (A) + (BC) and (AB) + (C)

Underwing (A) suitable for Galah, Corella and White Cockatoo

Underwing (B) suitable for Corella and White Cockatoo

Underwing (C) suitable for Corella, White and Pink Cockatoo

Underwing (AB) suitable for Pink Cockatoo

Underwing (BC) suitable for Galah

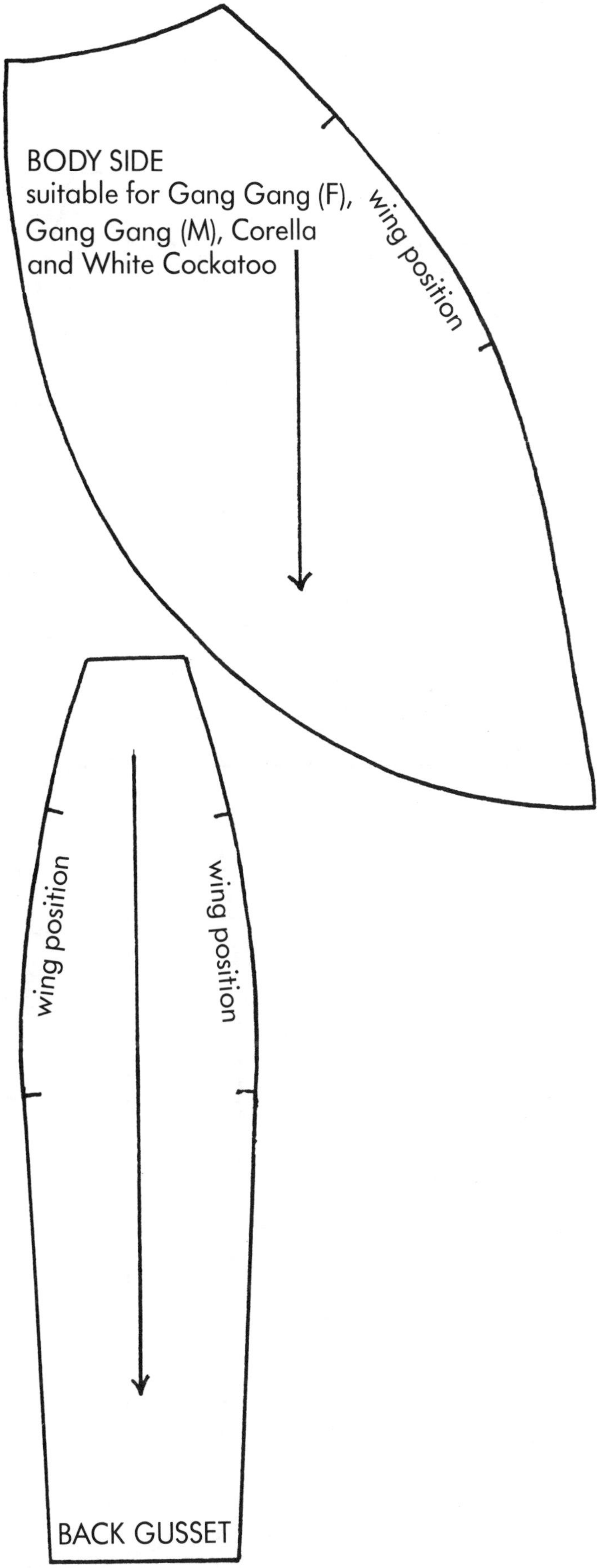
BODY SIDE
suitable for Gang Gang (F), Gang Gang (M), Corella and White Cockatoo
wing position
wing position
wing position
BACK GUSSET

suitable for Gang Gang (F) and (M), Corella and White Cockatoo

arrow indicates straight grain of fabric

seam allowance 5 mm (¼")

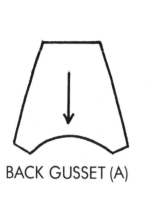

BACK GUSSET (A)

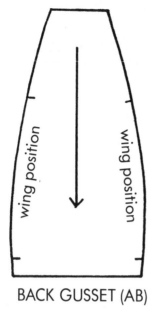

BACK GUSSET (AB)

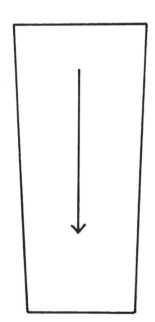

BACK GUSSET (B)

BACK GUSSET (C)

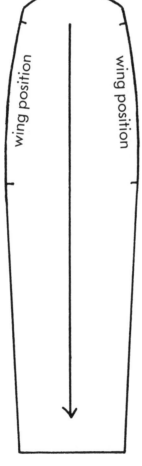

BACK GUSSET (BC)

Preliminary Joining Procedure

Step 1: Match the centre of the curved sides of Back Gusset (A) and Back Gusset (B) (Fig 1).

Step 2: Pin and stitch the pieces together (Fig. 2).

Step 3: Pin and sew Back Gusset (A) and B.G. (B) or Back Gusset (AB) to Back Gusset (C) (Fig. 3)

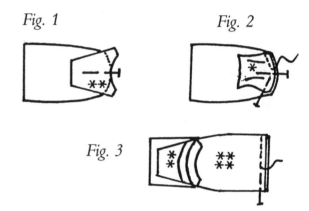

Fig. 1   Fig. 2

Fig. 3

✶✶ indicates wrong side of fabric

Note: The same method applies when joining Back Gusset (A) to B.G. (BC). Continue as for the Bird instructions.

Position wings between marks on Back Gusset

Back Gusset combinations are the same as for the Underwing

Back Gusset (AB) suitable for King Parrot (female)

Back Gusset (BC) suitable for Galah and Pink Cockatoo

Back Gusset (A) suitable for King Parrot (male), Galah and Pink Cockatoo

B.G. (B) suitable for King Parrot (male).

B.G. (C) suitable for King Parrot (male) and (female).

Preliminary Joining Procedure

Step 1: For each Body Side panel, pin and stitch a Body Side (A) piece to the corresponding Body Side (B) piece (Fig. 1).

Step 2: Pin and sew a Body Side (C) piece to the Body Side (A) and (B) pieces (Fig. 2)

The King Parrot (female) Body Side pieces are now ready to continue as for the Bird instructions.

Preliminary Joining Procedure

For each Body Side panel, pin and stitch a Body Side (C) piece to the corresponding Body Side (AB) piece (Fig. 1).

Continue as for the Bird instructions.

✱✱ indicates wrong side of fabric

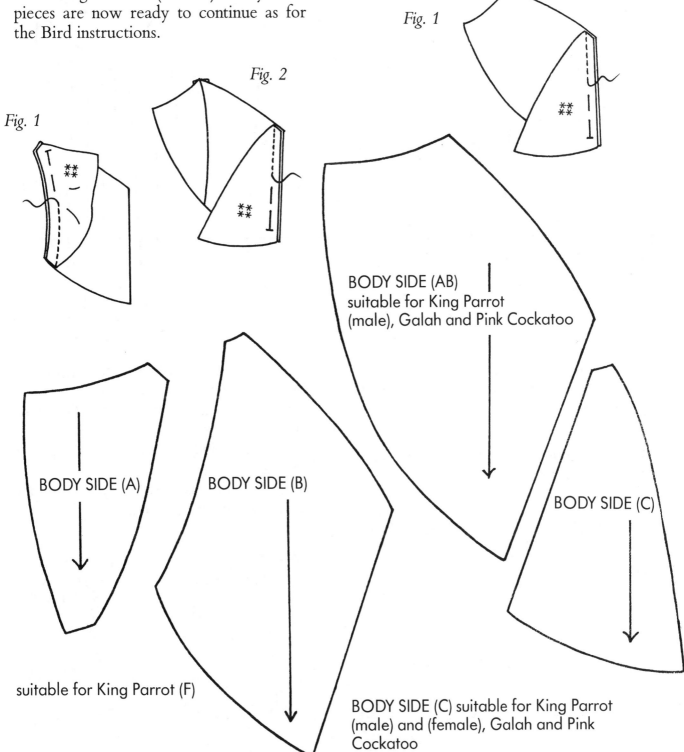

Fig. 1

Fig. 2

Fig. 1

BODY SIDE (AB)
suitable for King Parrot
(male), Galah and Pink Cockatoo

BODY SIDE (A)

BODY SIDE (B)

BODY SIDE (C)

suitable for King Parrot (F)

BODY SIDE (C) suitable for King Parrot
(male) and (female), Galah and Pink
Cockatoo

29

arrow indicates straight grain of fabric

Tailfront (A) and (B) Suitable for White and Pink Cockatoo and Corella

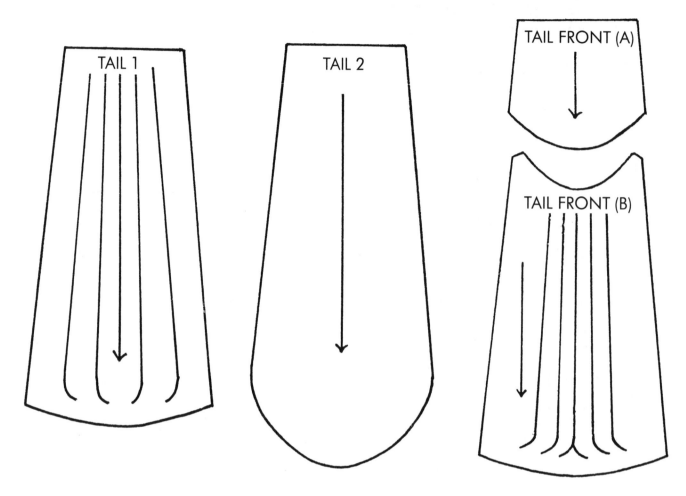

Tail 1 suitable for Gang Gang (F), Gang Gang (M), Corella, Galah, White and Pink Cockatoo

Tail 2 suitable for King Parrot (male) and King Parrot (female)

Feather details indicated by solid line, on Tail 1 and Tail Front (B)

✳✳ indicates wrong side of fabric

Preliminary Joining Procedure

Step 1: Match the centre of the curved side of the Tail Front (A) and Tail Front (B) pieces (Fig. 1).

Step 2: Pin and sew the pieces together (Fig. 2)

The Tail Front is now ready to continue with the Bird instructions.

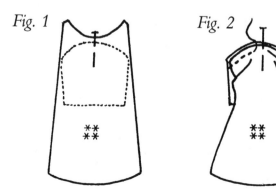

seam allowance 5 mm (¼″)

stitching guide indicated by dotted line

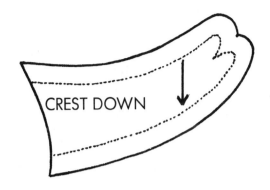

Preliminary Joining Procedure

Step 1: Using the dotted line as a stitching guide, sew a pair of Crest Down pieces together. Tie off all threads and clip the curves.

Step 2: Turn right side out and stuff. Refer to the Pink Cockatoo instructions, see step 5 and (Fig. 5) of the joining procedure below.

Crest Down suitable for White Cockatoo and as paper pattern for Pink Cockatoo

Preliminary Joining Procedure

Step 1: With right sides facing, pin and sew the Crest Down pieces together in the following order (A), (B), (C), (B), (A). By colour, this is as follows: white, red, white, red, white (Fig. 1). Iron the pieces so that the seam allowances fold towards the white pieces.

Step 2: With right sides facing, fold in half along the centre of piece (C). Make sure that the seams match, then pin securely. Tie off the threads from one side to the other for added stability (Fig. 2).

Step 3: Pin the Crest Down paper pattern onto the panel and draw around with a sharp tailor's chalk pencil or an ordinary pencil. Remove the paper pattern piece.

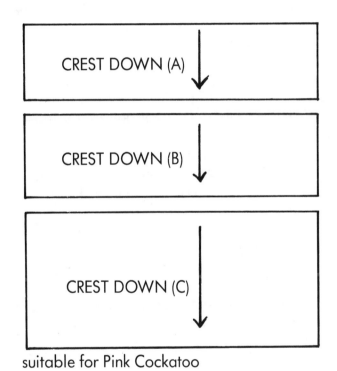

suitable for Pink Cockatoo

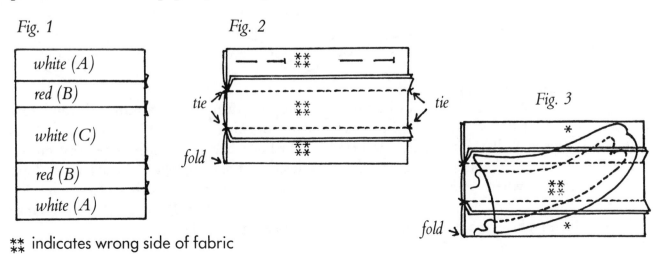

Fig. 1

| white (A) |
| red (B) |
| white (C) |
| red (B) |
| white (A) |

Fig. 2

tie / fold

Fig. 3

fold

✳✳ indicates wrong side of fabric

Do not cut out. Stitch 5 mm (¼″) away from the chalk/pencil line, leaving an opening for turning (Fig. 3). Restitch for strength and tie off all threads.

Step 4: Cut out carefully following the chalk/pencil line, making sure not to cut into the stitching. Clip into the tight corners (Fig. 4). Before turning, check the seams and put a few hand stitches in to secure the seam ends, if necessary. Turn and stuff.

Step 5: Turn under 5 mm (¼″) and sew the opening closed. Continue as for the Bird instructions. Position the crest on the head and stitch around twice, using a ladder stitch (Fig. 5).

Fig. 4

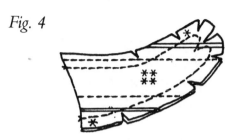

Fig. 5

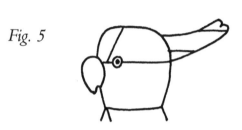

Crest Up pattern is suitable for the White Cockatoo and as a paper pattern for the Pink Cockatoo.

Follow the preliminary joining procedure below for the White Cockatoo, with Crest Up. The Pink Cockatoo with Crest Up instructions are on the opposite page.

Dotted line indicates stitching guide for Crest Up.

The thin solid lines indicate where to clip into the tight corners

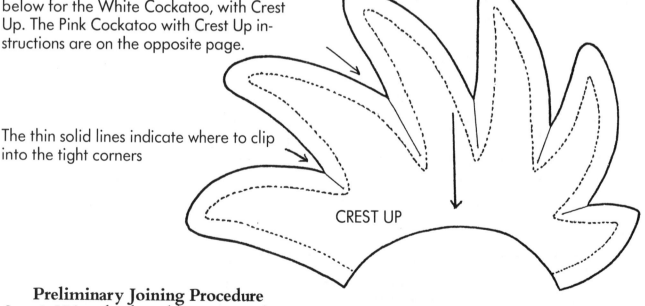

CREST UP

Preliminary Joining Procedure

Step 1: Using the dotted line as a stitching guide, sew a pair of Crest Up pieces together. Tie off all the threads, cut off the tips of the feathers and clip into the tight corners, where indicated on the pattern.

Step 2: Turn right side out and stuff.

Step 3: Turn under 5 mm (¼″) and sew the opening closed. Continue as for the Bird instructions. Position the crest on the head and sew in place. Stitch first along one side, then the other. Restitch. See (Fig. 5) of the Pink Cockatoo joining procedure.

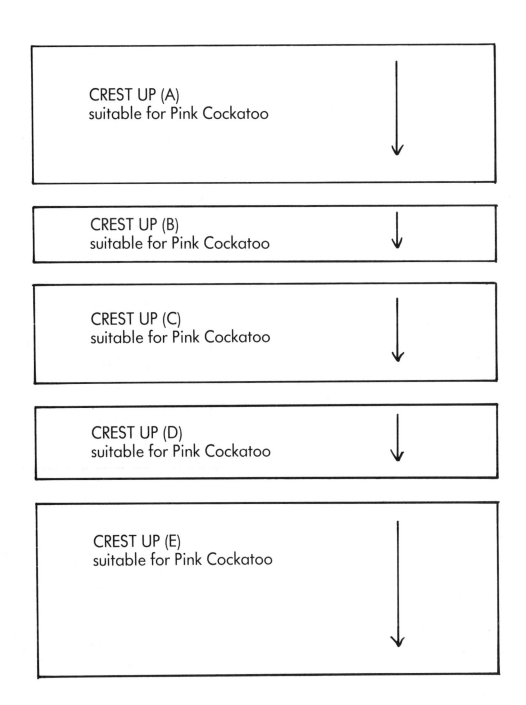

CREST UP (A)
suitable for Pink Cockatoo

CREST UP (B)
suitable for Pink Cockatoo

CREST UP (C)
suitable for Pink Cockatoo

CREST UP (D)
suitable for Pink Cockatoo

CREST UP (E)
suitable for Pink Cockatoo

Fig. 1

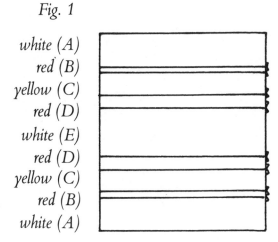

white (A)
red (B)
yellow (C)
red (D)
white (E)
red (D)
yellow (C)
red (B)
white (A)

Preliminary Joining Procedure

Step 1: With right sides facing, sew the Crest Up pieces together in the following order (A), (B), (C), (D), (E), (D), (C), (B), (A). By colour, this is as follows: white, red, yellow, red, white, red, yellow, red, white (Fig. 1). Iron the pieces so that the seam allowances fold towards the red pieces.

33

Step 2: With right sides facing, fold in half along the centre of the white Crest Up (E) piece. Make sure that the seams match, then pin securely. Tie off the threads from one side to the other for added stability (Fig. 2).

Step 3: Pin the Crest Up paper pattern onto the panel and draw around it with a sharp tailor's chalk pencil or an ordinary pencil. Remove the paper pattern piece. **Do not cut out.** Using the dotted line, which is on the paper pattern as a guide, sew approximately 5 mm (¼″) away from the chalk/pencil line. Leave an opening for turning (Fig. 3). Restitch for strength and tie off all threads.

Step 4: Cut out carefully following the chalk/pencil line. Making sure not to cut into the stitching, clip into the tight corners, as indicated on the paper pattern. Cut off the tips of the feathers (Fig. 4). Before turning, check the seams and put a few hand stitches in to secure the seam ends, if necessary. Carefully turn the crest right side out, pushing the feathers all the way out with a blunt-ended tool. Use the tool to push small amounts of stuffing into the feathers, then continue stuffing so that the crest is a little flat and not too bulky looking.

Step 5: Turn under 5 mm (¼″) and sew the opening closed using a whip stitch. The Pink Cockatoo crest is now ready to continue with the Bird instructions. Position the crest on the head and ladder stitch it in place. Sew first along one side then the other side. Stitch around again for strength (Fig. 5).

Draw lower machine sewing thread through to upper side of work. Tie threads into a knot and cut off.

Fig. 2

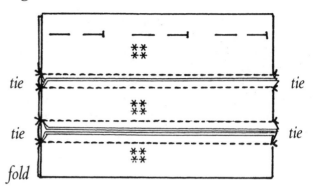

Fig. 3

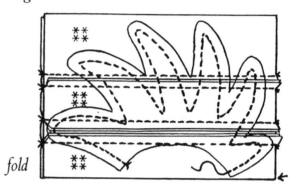

Fig. 4

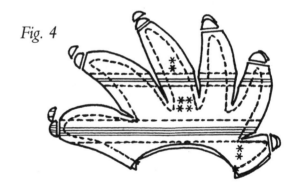

Fig. 5

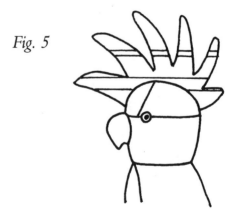

✶✶ indicates wrong side of fabric

34

BUTTERFLIES ON BARK
Inset: BUTTERFLIES ON QUILT

BIRDS IN TREE:

KING PARROT (MALE), MAJOR MITCHELL COCKATOO AND KING PARROT (FEMALE)

GALAH, CORELLA,
SULPHUR-CRESTED COCKATOO,
AND MAJOR MITCHELL COCKATOO

FIVE BIG CATS

CHEETAH AND TIGER

BIRD INSTRUCTIONS

METHOD FOR BIRDS

Ten different birds can be made from the one set of pattern pieces.

Male and female birds: Gang Gang Cockatoos and King Parrots.

Birds with their crest up or crest down: Sulphur-crested (White) Cockatoo and Major Mitchell (Pink) Cockatoo.

Plus a (Little White) Corella and a Galah.
  The illustrations which accompany the directions on this and the following pages show the female Gang Gang Cockatoo pattern shapes. However, the method used to make the toy is the same for all the other, different variations. For all the other birds, follow the preliminary joining procedure instructions given in the pattern section. Then continue as follows:

Head

1. With right sides facing and the Beak pieces underneath, pin a Head piece to each Beak piece (Fig. 1). Stitch carefully 5 mm (¼″) from the edge. Tack by hand first or backstitch the seam instead of machine stitching if you wish.

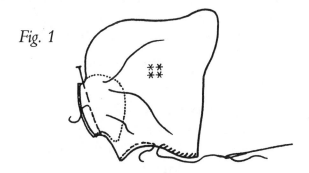

Fig. 1

Neck edge stay stitching not shown in following illustrations

2. Pin the pair of head sections together, carefully matching the beak seams. (See the Hints section on page 3 for information about using the tied sewing threads to help match seams.) Stitch (Fig. 2). Cut off the tip of the beak and clip the curves and tight corners. Turn and stuff.

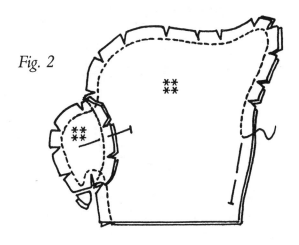

Fig. 2

Body

1. Cut two lengths of 12 mm (½″) wide elastic, 4 cm (1½″) long. Pin one end of each piece of elastic to the right side of the Centre Front piece, where marked on the upper edge (Fig. 1). Stitch 2–3 mm (⅛″) from the edge across both pieces of elastic.

Fig. 1

2. Pin the other ends of the elastic to the lower edge of the Centre Front, using the marks as a guide (Fig. 2). Stitch 2–3 mm (⅛″) from the edge across both pieces of elastic, thus forming the loops for the feet.

Fig. 2

3. With right sides facing, pin the upper edge of the Centre Front piece to the straight edge of the Chest piece (Fig. 3). Sew 5 mm (¼″) from the edge.

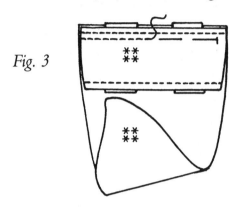

Fig. 3

4. Pin the upper straight edge of the Lower Front piece to the lower edge of the Centre Front piece (Fig. 4). Stitch 5 mm (¼″) from the edge.

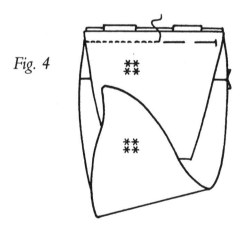

Fig. 4

5. Overcast the front gusset seams by catching the raw edges of the seam allowances together. Using a zig zag stitch, sew over the edge, or as close as possible to the edge as your sewing machine will allow (Fig. 5). Alternatively, whip stitch by hand to stop the fabric fraying.

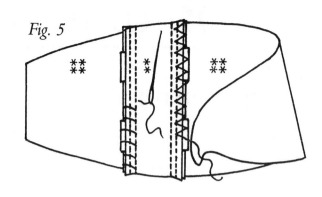

Fig. 5

6. Using a 5 mm (¼″) seam allowance, sew the Wing pieces together in pairs. Leave the wing open on the straight edge to allow for turning (Fig. 6). Cut off the wing-tip and clip the curves. Turn and stuff each wing so that it is not quite full and appears flat, not bulky. Sew the straight edges together, 2–3 mm (⅛″) from the edge (Fig. 7).

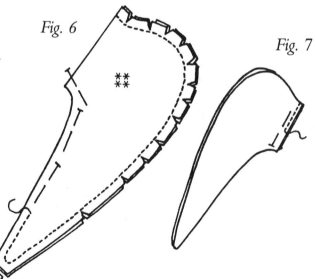

Fig. 6

Fig. 7

Note: For the male King Parrot, for each wing, pair together a Wing piece and an Upper wing panel. For the rest of the birds it will be an Underwing panel and a Wing piece for each wing.

7. Attach the wings to the Back Gusset one at a time, where marked. (See the pattern section.) Tack by hand then stitch 3–4 mm (⅛″) from the edge (Fig. 8). Check to make sure that both straight edges of each wing are caught in the seam.

Note: The Wing piece, or the Upperwing as in the case of the male King Parrot, is facing the Back Gusset, not the Underwing panel. Stitch with the right side of the Back Gusset facing up and the wing on top.

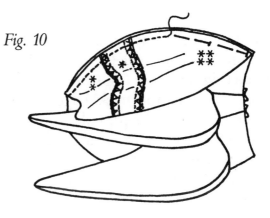

Fig. 10

tacking shown

Fig. 8

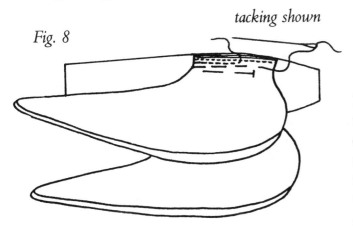

8. With right sides facing, pin the Body Side pieces to the Back Gusset so that the wings are between the gusset and the side pieces (Fig. 9). Tack, then stitch, 5 mm (¼″) from the edge, taking care when sewing through the multiple thicknesses. If you find it too difficult to stitch the multiple thicknesses by machine, sew the seam by hand using a back stitch.

10. Pin and sew a pair of Tail pieces together, leaving the straight top edge open for turning. Clip the corners off, close to the stitching. Turn and stuff so that the tail is flat and not bulky. Stitch the opening closed, 2 mm (¹⁄₁₆″) from the edges. Attach the tail to the body, pinning it to the lower edge of the Back Gusset. Stitch 2–3 mm (⅛″) from the edge. Check to make sure all the straight edges have been caught in the seam (Fig. 11).

Fig. 11

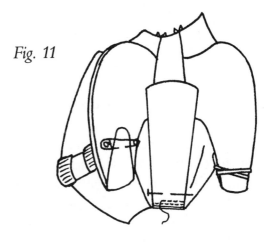

Fig. 9

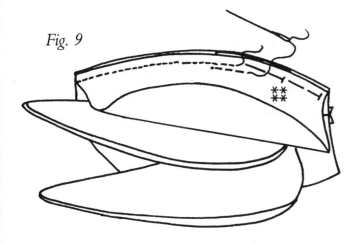

9. Pin and sew the front gusset panel to the front edge of one Body Side piece (Fig. 10).

Note: The joined Tail Front pieces face upwards when the tail is attached to the Back Gusset.

11. Stay stitch the neck edge, using hand whip stitching or straight machine sewing (Fig. 11). Bend the wing tips up. secure with elastic bands, small safety pins or tie with thread. (Do not leave elastic bands on for long periods.)

12. Pin the other front gusset edge to the remaining Body Side edge, having the tail enclosed (Fig. 12). Tack and stitch, starting 2.5 cm (1") from the neck edge. Make sure that the elastic loops, tail and wings do not get caught in the seam. Turn the body over and check the seam from the other side. Unpick and restitch, if necessary. If you find the seam too difficult to stitch by machine, sew by hand using a back stitch.

Fig. 12

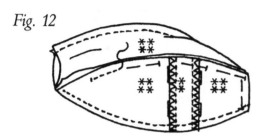

✳✳ indicates wrong side of fabric

Completing the Toy

1. To turn the body right side out, carefully pull the wings and tail through the neck opening, one by one. Start by pulling the shoulder of one wing, easing it all the way out. Repeat the procedure for the other wing. Turn completely through by grasping the end of the tail and pull it through the neck opening also. Remove the elastic bands, thread or safety pins. Check all the seams. The seams may need to be restitched at the neck edge by hand if they have come undone. Sew the final 2.5 cm (1") of the body side seam using ladder stitch.

2. Stuff the body. Join the stuffed head to the body using ladder stitch. Have the head looking straight ahead or a little to one side. Add more stuffing before completely closing the opening, to make the neck firmer. Sew around again for strength (Fig. 1).

Illustration shows male and female Gang Gang Cockatoo

Fig. 1

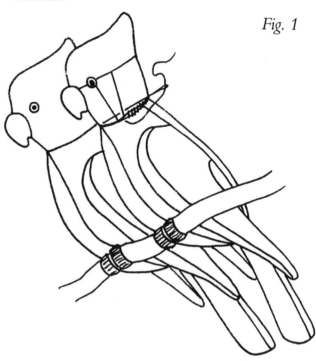

Note: Refer to the pattern section for directions concerning the construction and attachment of the crests (up or down) of the White and Pink Cockatoos.

3. Sew 'joggle' eyes in position on each side of the head (Fig. 1). If the toy is for a very small child who may chew and swallow such small eyes, then embroider instead using satin stitch.

BIG CATS

Big cats are admired for their power, grace and majesty, as well as their beautifully patterned coats.

Realistic, yet cuddly, ten different big cats can be made using this set of multiple-choice pattern pieces. The big cats are as follows: Puma, Jaguar, Black Panther, Cheetah, Leopard, Lioness, Lion, White Tiger, Snow Leopard and Tiger.

Each Big Cat measures approximately 45.5 cm–51 cm (18"–20") in length and is 29 cm (11½") tall from the base to the tip of the ears. The measurements may vary depending on the type of fabric used. The big cats have 'safety' eyes and noses (or a nose embroidered with satin stitch). The whiskers are made from hat elastic and, therefore, are not a danger to a child's eyes. The toy can be made using one of the many commercially available animal-print designs, or solid colour, fake fur fabrics. Or, you can make your own unique, hand-painted toy using fabric paints on tracksuit (fleecy) fabric.

Suitable fabrics: Velvet, velour, fleecy (tracksuit) fabric, used with either side as the right side, or short pile fur fabric. Long pile fur of a matching colour is also needed for the tail tip of the Lion and Lioness as well as for the mane of the Lion.

MATERIALS FOR EACH BIG CAT

Refer to the individual lists for the colours needed.
- *1 pair of 15 mm (½") crystal 'safety' eyes (with round pupils) and 2 washers*
- *1 x 21 mm (1") 'safety' nose (triangular 'rabbit' nose) and washer, or embroidery floss*
- *1 metre (40") hat elastic (1.4 m [56"] if using fur fabric)*
- *1 skein of black embroidery floss. (This is sufficient for many toys.)*
- *Approximately 600 g–800 g (20–27 oz) polyester fibre filling*
- *Black fabric paint — shiny or iridescent (plus brown for Jaguar) for handpainted toys. (Paint the fabric pieces **before** stitching.)*
- *For all the Big Cats, except the Snow Leopard and Tiger, you will need a 50 cm x 152 cm (20" x 60") piece of the required colour or 'animal print' design of fabric*
- *For the Tiger you will need a 40 cm x 152 cm (16" x 60") piece of tiger-striped fur fabric or solid-colour non-fur fabric. (Paint stripes on prior to stitching.) Plus, a 45 cm x 60 cm (18" x 24") piece of white tiger-striped (or plain white) fur fabric or white non-fur fabric. The Snow Leopard requires approximately the same amounts of fabric. Remember, use only fur with fur and fleecy with fleecy for these two Cats.*

BIG CAT PATTERN LISTS

Before starting to make your toy, please read carefully through the section on HINTS, for the following information:
- General toymaking equipment and requirements
- Tracing the pattern pieces onto paper
- The selection and cutting of fabric
- Transferring markings onto fabric
- Painting with fabric paints
- Stitching methods and techniques for finishing raw edges
- The importance of tying off threads

- Seam matching techniques
- Turning the toy right side out and stuffing

Note: Remember only one of each paper pattern piece need be cut out. Mark the paper pattern with all the markings, including the fabric-painting guide lines and the names of the other Big Cats that the piece is suitable for. (You may want to make a different Big Cat in the future and this saves you from tracing the piece a second time.) When referring to the lists of pattern pieces, make note of the **name**, **number** and **(letter)** given for each piece. This ensures that the correct piece is selected.

When a direction is given to cut two of a particular colour, this means that a pair of fabric pieces are needed. Thus, if you are cutting on a single thickness of fabric, turn the paper pattern over so that it is reversed (R). Keep the straight grain arrows pointing the same way for all the pieces. (See the pattern layout diagram.)

Puma (Mountain lion)
Head Side front 1 cut 2 tan
Head Side Back 1 cut 2 tan
Cheek 1 cut 2 tan
Chin cut 1 tan
Head Gusset 1 cut 1 tan
Ear 1 cut 4 tan
Front Gusset cut 1 tan
Body Side Front cut 2 tan
Body Side Back cut 2 tan
Inside Leg cut 2 tan
Body Base cut 1 tan
Tail 1 cut 2 tan
Eyes gold or yellow
Nose pink
Whiskers white

Jaguar
Head Side Front 1 cut 2 tan (rings)
Head Side Back 1 cut 2 tan (rings)

Cheek 1 cut 2 tan (rings)
Chin cut 1 tan (rings)
Head Gusset 1 cut 1 tan (rings)
Ear 1 cut 4 tan (rings)
Front Gusset cut 1 tan (rings)
Body Side Front cut 2 tan (rings)
Body Side Back cut 2 tan (rings)
Inside Leg cut 2 tan (rings)
Body Base cut 1 tan (rings)
Tail 1 cut 2 tan (rings)
Eyes gold or yellow
Nose pink
Whiskers white

Black Panther
Head Side Front 1 cut 2 black
Head Side Back 1 cut 2 black
Cheek 1 cut 2 black
Chin cut 1 black
Head Gusset 1 cut 1 black
Ear 1 cut 4 black
Front Gusset cut 1 black
Body Side Front cut 2 black
Body Side Back cut 2 black
Inside Leg cut 2 black
Body Base cut 1 black
Tail 1 cut 2 black
Eyes gold
Nose black
Whiskers black

Cheetah
Head Side Front 1 cut 2 tan (spots)
Head Side Back 1 cut 2 tan (spots)
Cheek 1 cut 2 tan (striped)
Chin cut 1 tan
Head Gusset 1 cut 1 tan (spots)
Ear 1 cut 4 tan
Front Gusset cut 1 tan (spots)
Body Side Front cut 2 tan (spots)
Body Side Back cut 2 tan (spots)
Inside Leg cut 2 tan spots
Body Base cut 1 tan (spots)
Tail 1 cut 2 tan (spots)
Eyes orange or gold

Nose black
Whiskers white

Note: In the lists below, when a colour is given, followed by the word 'fur', this refers to long-pile fur. For the other pattern pieces, only a colour is given. Any of the previously mentioned fabrics can be used, except long-pile fur fabric.

Leopard
Head Side Front 1 cut 2 tan (spots)
Head Side Back 1 cut 2 tan (spots)
Cheek 1 cut 2 tan (spots)
Chin cut 1 tan (spots)
Head Gusset 1 cut 1 tan (spots)
Ear 1 cut 4 tan (spots)
Front Gusset cut 1 tan (spots)
Body Side Front cut 2 tan (spots)
Body Side Back cut 2 tan (spots)
Inside Leg cut 2 tan (spots)
Body Base cut 1 tan (spots)
Tail 1 cut 2 tan (spots)
Eyes gold or yellow
Nose black or pink
Whiskers black or white

Lioness
Head Side Front 2 cut 2 tan
Head Side Back 2 cut 2 tan
Cheek 2 cut 2 tan
Chin cut 1 tan
Head Gusset 1 cut 1 tan
Ear 1 cut 4 tan
Front Gusset cut 1 tan
Body Side Front cut 2 tan
Body Side Back cut 2 tan
Inside Leg cut 2 tan
Body Base cut 1 tan
Tail 2(A) cut 2 tan
Tail 2(B) cut 2 tan Fur
Eyes gold or yellow
Nose black or pink
Whiskers white

Lion
Head Side Front 2(A) cut 2 tan
Head Side Front 2(B) cut 2 tan Fur
Head Side Back 2 cut 2 tan Fur
Cheek 2 cut 2 tan
Chin cut 1 tan
Head Gusset 1(A) cut 1 tan
Head Gusset 1(B) cut 1 tan Fur
Ear 1 cut 4 tan
Front Gusset (A) cut 1 tan Fur
Front Gusset (B) cut 1 tan
Body Side Front (A) cut 2 tan Fur
Body Side Front (B) cut 2 tan
Body Side Back cut 2 tan
Inside Leg cut 2 tan
Body Base cut 1 tan
Tail 2 (A) cut 2 tan
Tail 2 (B) cut 2 tan Fur
Eyes gold or yellow
Nose black or pink
Whiskers black or white

Note: For the White Tiger, plain white fabric can be used instead of striped white fabric.

White Tiger
Head Side Front 3 cut 2 white (stripes)
Head Side Back 3 cut 2 white (stripes)
Cheek 1 cut 2 white (stripes)
Chin cut 1 white (stripes)
Head Gusset 2 cut 1 white (stripes)
Ear 2 cut 4 white (stripes)
Front Gusset cut 1 white (stripes)
Body Side Front cut 2 white (stripes)
Body Side Back cut 2 white (stripes)
Inside Leg cut 2 white (stripes)
Body Base cut 1 white (stripes)
Tail 1 cut 2 white (stripes)
Eyes blue
Nose pink
Whiskers white

Tiger

Head Side Front 3 (A) cut 2 white (stripes)
Head Side Front 3 (B) cut 2 rust (stripes)
Head Side Front 3 (C) cut 2 white (stripes)
Head Side Back 3 cut 2 rust (stripes)
Cheek 1 (A) cut 2 white or white (stripes)
Cheek 1 (B) cut 2 rust (stripes)
Chin cut 1 white or white (stripes)
Head Gusset 2 (A) cut 1 rust (stripes)
Head Gusset 2 (B) cut 1 white (stripes)
Head Gusset 2 (C) cut 1 rust (stripes)
Ear 2 cut 2 white or white (stripes)
Ear 2 (A) cut 2 rust (stripes)
Ear 2 (B) cut 2 white
Front Gusset (C) cut 2 rust (stripes)
Front Gusset (D) cut 1 white (stripes)
Body Side Front cut 2 rust (stripes)
Body Side Back cut 2 rust (stripes)
Inside Leg (A) cut 2 rust (stripes)
Inside Leg (B) cut 2 white (stripes)
Body Base cut 1 white (stripes)
Tail 1 cut 1 rust (stripes)
Tail 1 cut 1 white (stripes) reversed
Eyes gold or yellow
Nose pink
Whiskers white

Snow Leopard

Head Side Front 1 cut 2 grey (rings)
Head Side Back 1 cut 2 grey (rings)
Cheek 1 (A) cut 2 white
Cheek 1 (B) cut 2 grey or grey (rings)
Chin cut 1 white
Head Gusset 1 cut 1 grey (rings)
Ear 2 cut 2 white
Ear 2 (A) cut 2 grey or grey (rings)
Ear 2 (B) cut 2 white
Front Gusset (C) cut 2 grey (rings)
Front Gusset (D) cut 1 white
Body Side Front cut 2 grey (rings)
Body Side Back cut 2 grey (rings)
Inside Leg (A) cut 2 grey (rings)
Inside Leg (B) cut 2 white
Body Base cut 1 white
Tail 1 cut 2 grey (rings)
Eyes blue, gold or yellow
Nose pink
Whiskers black or white

Big Cat Pattern Section

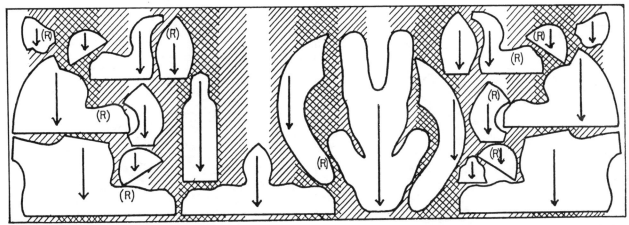

The pattern layout above represents Leopard pattern pieces on leopard-print fur fabric. The fabric is made up of three tonal (hatched) areas — light, medium and dark tan. Notice how the paper pattern pieces are placed so that each pair of shapes (R = the reversed paper pattern piece) has the same tonal value. If your piece of fur fabric is different to that illustrated, rearrange the pieces accordingly. Remember that the chest, inner leg and tummy of the leopard are slightly lighter in colour than the rest of the body. Use the same pattern layout for the Puma, Jaguar, Black Panther and Cheetah. Change the pattern pieces and use the same placements for the Lioness, Lion and White Tiger. (Spots are not shown in the illustration.)

Note: The layout is for 50 cm x 152 cm (20" x 60") fabric.

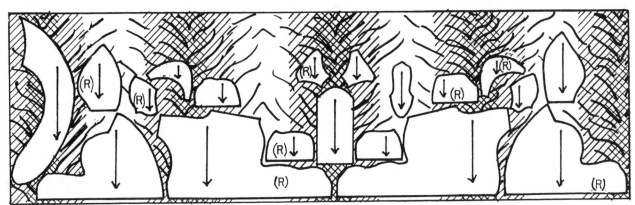

The pattern layout above represents Tiger pattern pieces on tan, tiger-striped fur fabric. The fabric is made up of three tonal (hatched) areas — light, medium and dark. Notice how the paper pattern pieces are placed so that each pair of shapes (R = reversed paper pattern piece) has the same tonal value. If your piece of fur fabric is different to that illustrated, rearrange the pieces accordingly. (Illustration shows stripes.) The remaining Tiger paper pattern pieces should be arranged on plain white fur fabric or tiger-striped fur fabric. Place the head pieces so that the stripes follow the same directions as the painted Tiger. Have the stripes central on the body base and give the ears a dark tip. Remember, the printed stripe on the backing is different to the actual position on the fur side. For the Snow Leopard and White Tiger, adapt the layouts illustrated.

Hand-painted Big Cat coat marking guidelines

When painting, use the larger spots and rings on the body pieces.

CHEETAH

tan

black

black

black

SNOW LEOPARD

grey

black

arrow indicates straight grain of fabric and stroke of fur

eye painting guideline is for Cheetah only

ear position

eye position

HEAD SIDE BACK 1

HEAD SIDE FRONT 1

suitable for Puma, Jaguar, Black Panther, Cheetah, Leopard and Snow Leopard

Tiger stripes are shown on all the
necessary pieces.

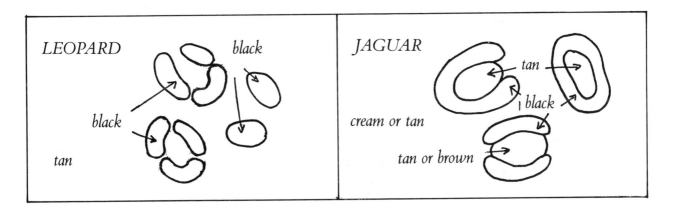

LEOPARD

black

black

tan

JAGUAR

tan

black

cream or tan

tan or brown

seam allowance 8 mm (⅓″)

arrow indicates straight grain of fabric
and stroke of fur

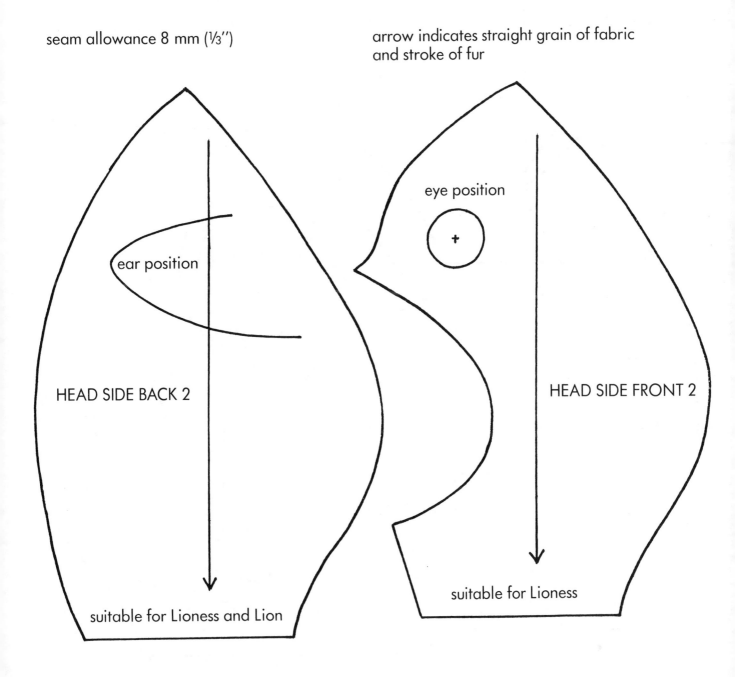

ear position

HEAD SIDE BACK 2

suitable for Lioness and Lion

eye position

HEAD SIDE FRONT 2

suitable for Lioness

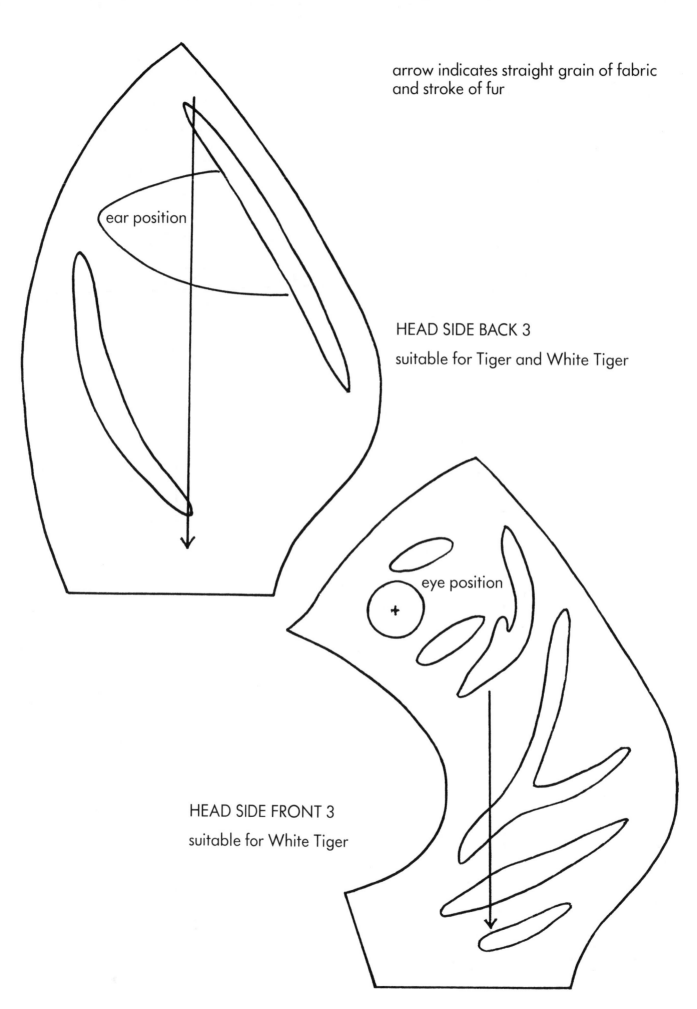

arrow indicates straight grain of fabric
and stroke of fur

ear position

HEAD SIDE BACK 3

suitable for Tiger and White Tiger

eye position

+

HEAD SIDE FRONT 3

suitable for White Tiger

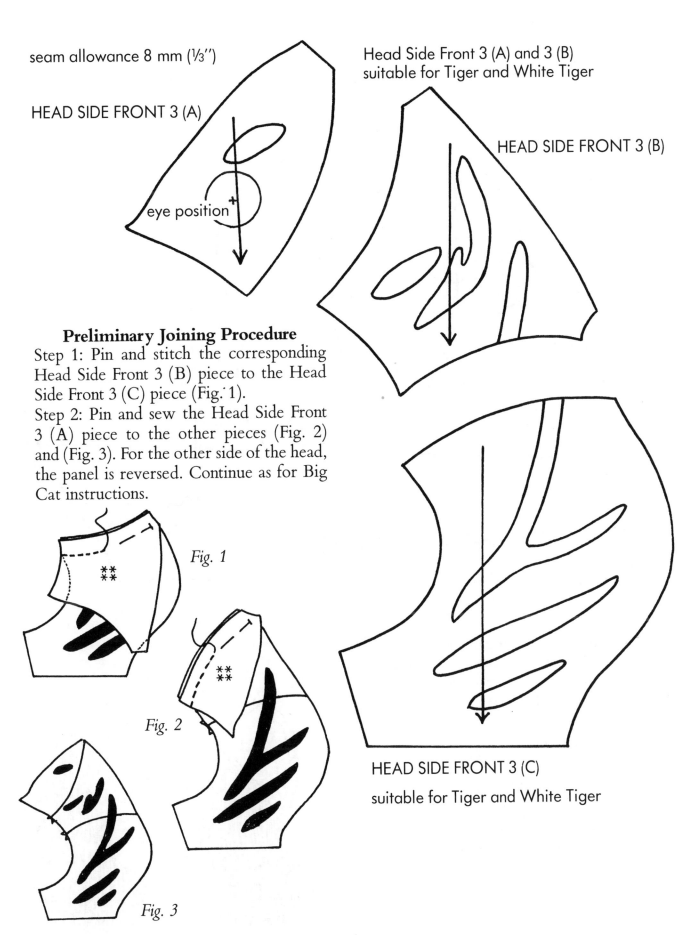

seam allowance 8 mm (⅓″)

HEAD SIDE FRONT 3 (A)

Head Side Front 3 (A) and 3 (B)
suitable for Tiger and White Tiger

HEAD SIDE FRONT 3 (B)

eye position

Preliminary Joining Procedure

Step 1: Pin and stitch the corresponding
Head Side Front 3 (B) piece to the Head
Side Front 3 (C) piece (Fig. 1).

Step 2: Pin and sew the Head Side Front
3 (A) piece to the other pieces (Fig. 2)
and (Fig. 3). For the other side of the head,
the panel is reversed. Continue as for Big
Cat instructions.

Fig. 1

Fig. 2

Fig. 3

HEAD SIDE FRONT 3 (C)

suitable for Tiger and White Tiger

✱✱ indicates wrong side of fabric

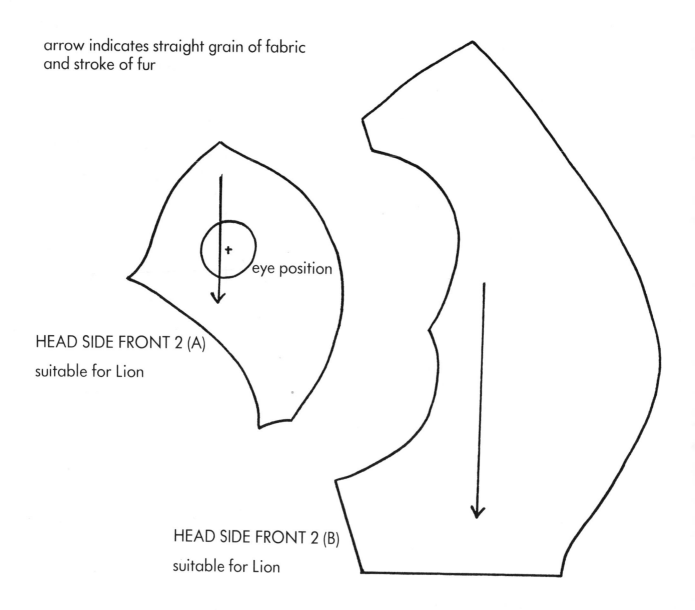

arrow indicates straight grain of fabric
and stroke of fur

eye position

HEAD SIDE FRONT 2 (A)

suitable for Lion

HEAD SIDE FRONT 2 (B)

suitable for Lion

Preliminary Joining Procedure

Step 1: For both sides of the head, pin and stitch the correct Head Side Front 2 (A) piece to the 2 (B) piece (Fig. 1) and (Fig. 2).

Step 2: Restitch from other side. Continue as for Big Cat instructions.

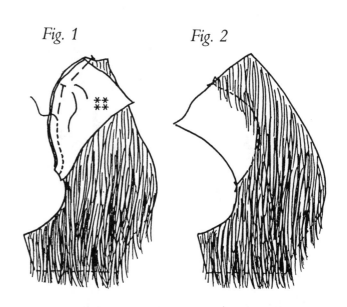

Fig. 1   *Fig. 2*

✳✳ indicates wrong side of fabric

seam allowance 8 mm (⅓″)

⚬ indicates position of whiskers

CHEEK 1

suitable for Puma, Jaguar, Black Panther, Cheetah, Leopard and White Tiger

Painting guideline suitable for Cheetah only

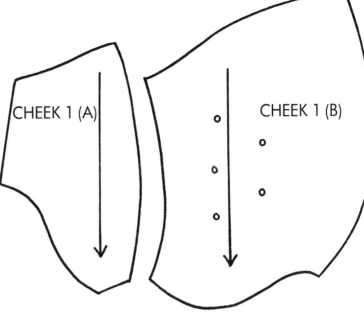

CHEEK 1 (A)

CHEEK 1 (B)

suitable for Snow Leopard and Tiger

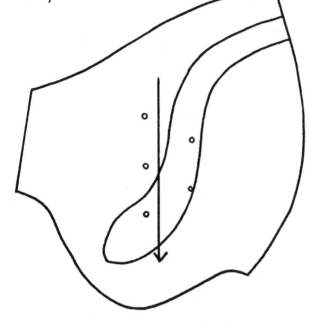

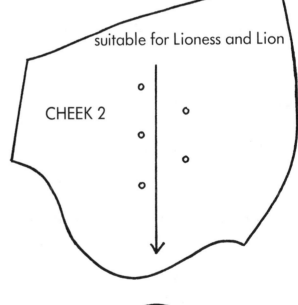

suitable for Lioness and Lion

CHEEK 2

Preliminary Joining Procedure

Step 1: Pin and stitch Cheek 1 (A) to Cheek 1 (B) (Fig. 1). The Cheek should resemble that illustrated (Fig. 2).

Step 2: Repeat procedure for the other Cheek pieces.

Continue as for the Big Cat instructions.

Fig. 1   *Fig. 2*

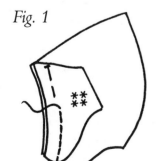

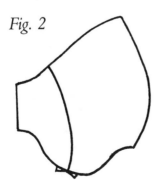

✳✳ indicates wrong side of fabric

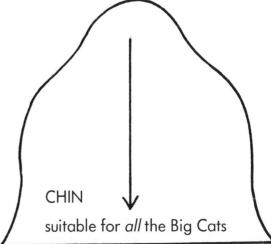

CHIN

suitable for *all* the Big Cats

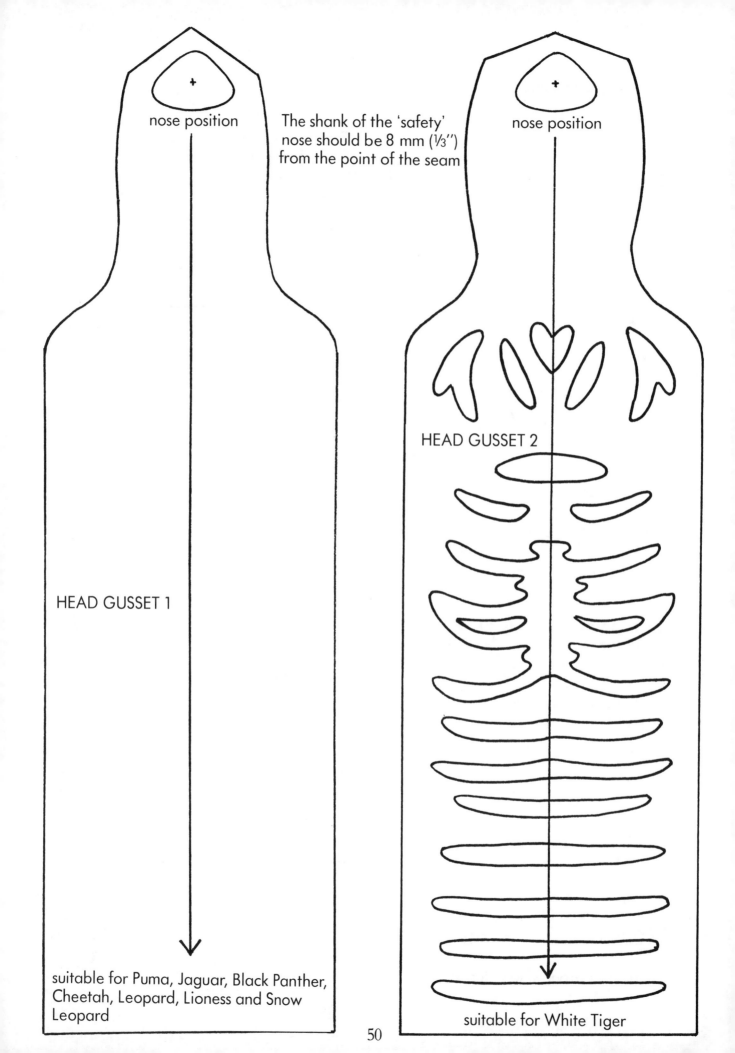

nose position

The shank of the 'safety' nose should be 8 mm (⅓″) from the point of the seam

nose position

HEAD GUSSET 2

HEAD GUSSET 1

suitable for Puma, Jaguar, Black Panther, Cheetah, Leopard, Lioness and Snow Leopard

50

suitable for White Tiger

HEAD GUSSET 1 (B)

suitable for Lion

seam allowance 8 mm (⅓″)

The shank of the 'safety' nose should be 8 mm (⅓″) from the point of the seam

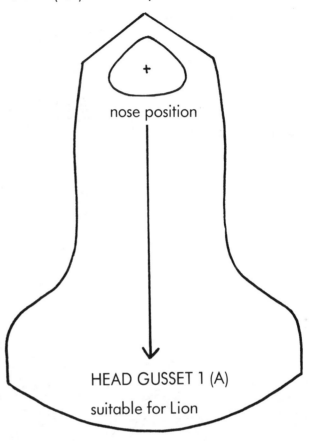

nose position

HEAD GUSSET 1 (A)

suitable for Lion

Preliminary Joining Procedure

Step 1: Matching the centre of the curved sides (Fig. 1), pin Head Gusset 1 (A) to 1 (B).

Step 2: Continue pinning and stitch (Fig. 2).

Step 3: Restitch from the other side. The panel should resemble (Fig. 3). Continue as for Big Cat instructions.

Fig. 1

Fig. 2

Fig. 3

✷✷ indicates wrong side of fabric

Preliminary Joining Procedure

Step 1: Matching the centres as shown, (Fig. 1), pin and stitch Head Gusset 2 (B) to 2 (A).

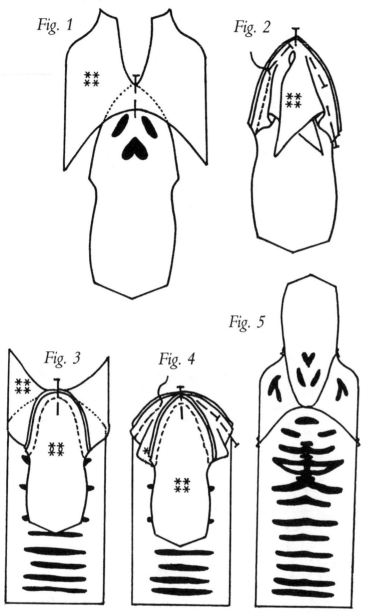

Fig. 1

Fig. 2

Fig. 3

Fig. 4

Fig. 5

Step 2: Matching the centres, pin the joined Head Gusset 2 (A) and 2 (B) pieces to the Head Gusset 2 (C) piece (Fig. 3).
Step 3: Continue pinning then stitch the seam. Tack first, if necessary (Fig. 4).
The completed Head Gusset panel should resemble that illustrated (Fig. 5). Continue as for the Big Cat instructions.

✱✱ indicates wrong side of fabric

seam allowance 8 mm (⅓″)

The shank of the 'safety' nose should be 8 mm (⅓″) from the point of the seam

HEAD GUSSET 2 (A)

suitable for Tiger

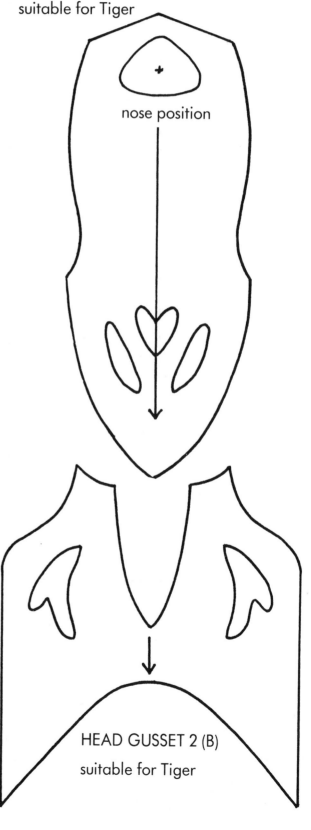

nose position

HEAD GUSSET 2 (B)

suitable for Tiger

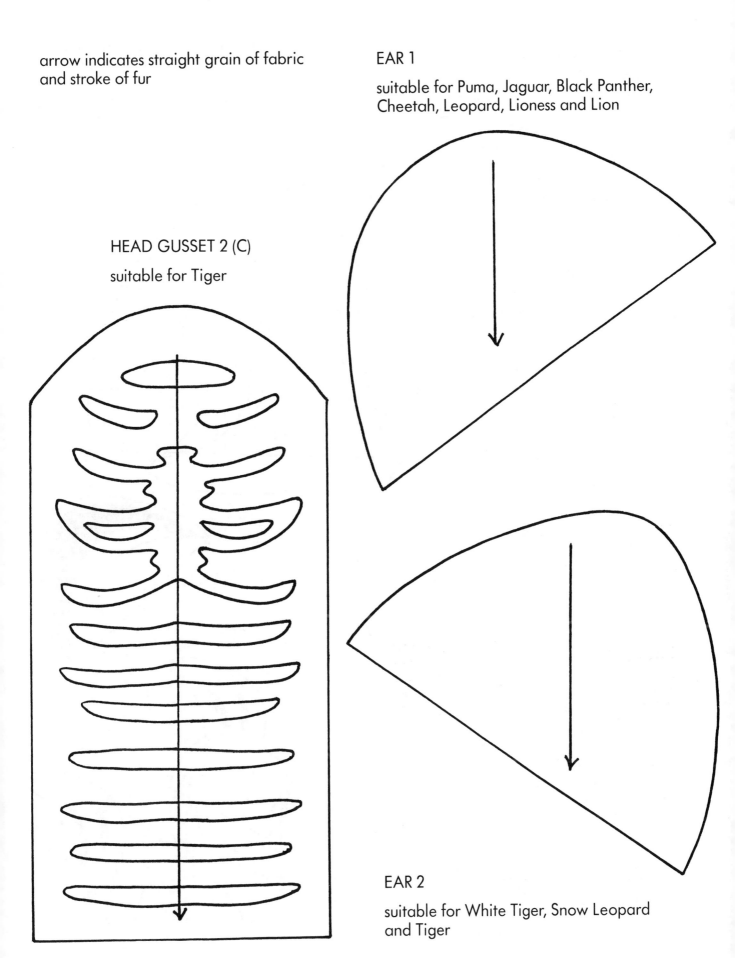

arrow indicates straight grain of fabric and stroke of fur

EAR 1

suitable for Puma, Jaguar, Black Panther, Cheetah, Leopard, Lioness and Lion

HEAD GUSSET 2 (C)

suitable for Tiger

EAR 2

suitable for White Tiger, Snow Leopard and Tiger

53

arrow indicates straight grain of fabric and stroke of fur

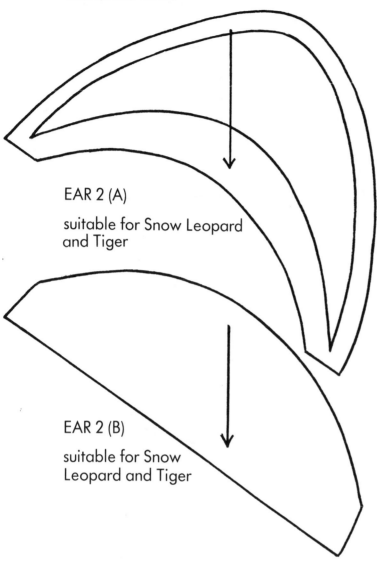

EAR 2 (A)

suitable for Snow Leopard and Tiger

EAR 2 (B)

suitable for Snow Leopard and Tiger

Preliminary Joining Procedure

Step 1: Matching the centres, pin Ear 2 (A) to 2 (B) (Fig. 1). Pin in the middle, then ends and in between.

Step 2: Stitch (Fig. 2). The Ear should resemble (Fig. 3). Repeat for the other Ear pieces.

Continue as for Big Cat instructions.

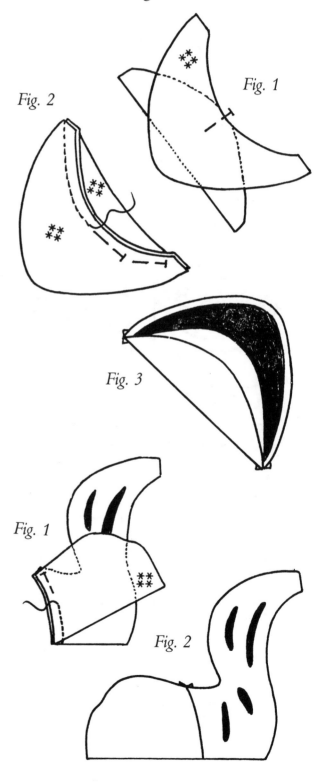

Fig. 2

Fig. 1

Fig. 3

Fig. 1

Fig. 2

Preliminary Joining Procedure

Step 1: Pin and stitch Inside Leg (A) to (B) (Fig. 1). The Inside Leg should resemble (Fig. 2).

Step 2: Repeat for the other pieces.

Continue as for the Big Cat instructions.

Inside Leg (A) and Inside Leg (B) are illustrated on the opposite page.

✶✶ indicates wrong side of fabric

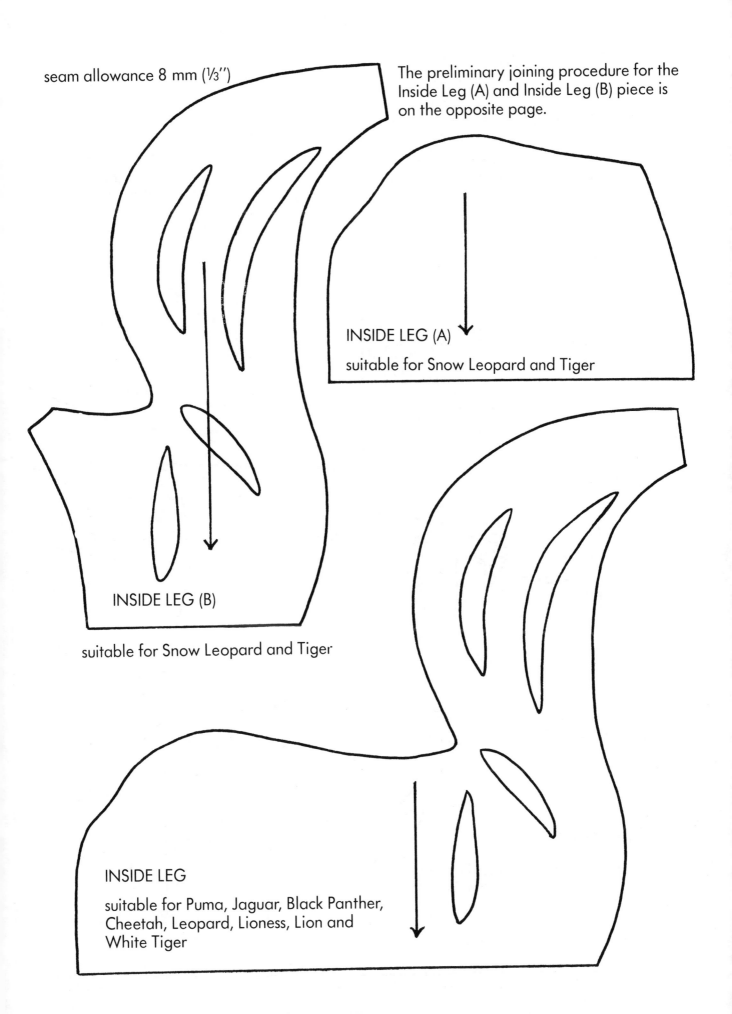

seam allowance 8 mm (⅓'')

The preliminary joining procedure for the Inside Leg (A) and Inside Leg (B) piece is on the opposite page.

INSIDE LEG (A)

suitable for Snow Leopard and Tiger

INSIDE LEG (B)

suitable for Snow Leopard and Tiger

INSIDE LEG

suitable for Puma, Jaguar, Black Panther, Cheetah, Leopard, Lioness, Lion and White Tiger

To make a paper pattern

Step 1: Trace the part of the Body Side Front illustrated on the opposite page, on to paper. Include all the markings.

Step 2: Trace the part of the Body Side Front illustrated on this page. Place the paper up against a window so that the light shines through. Transfer the markings to the other side.

Step 3: Cut out the paper pattern so that it resembles the small shape illustrated.

Step 3:

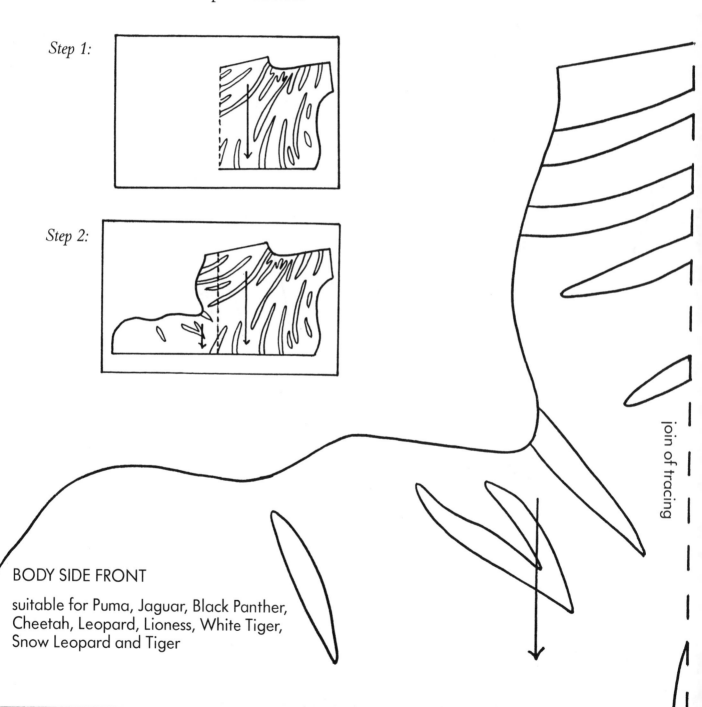

Step 1:

Step 2:

join of tracing

BODY SIDE FRONT

suitable for Puma, Jaguar, Black Panther, Cheetah, Leopard, Lioness, White Tiger, Snow Leopard and Tiger

arrow indicates straight grain of fabric
and stroke of fur

seam allowance 8 mm (⅓")

BODY SIDE FRONT

suitable for all the Big Cats except Lion

join of tracing

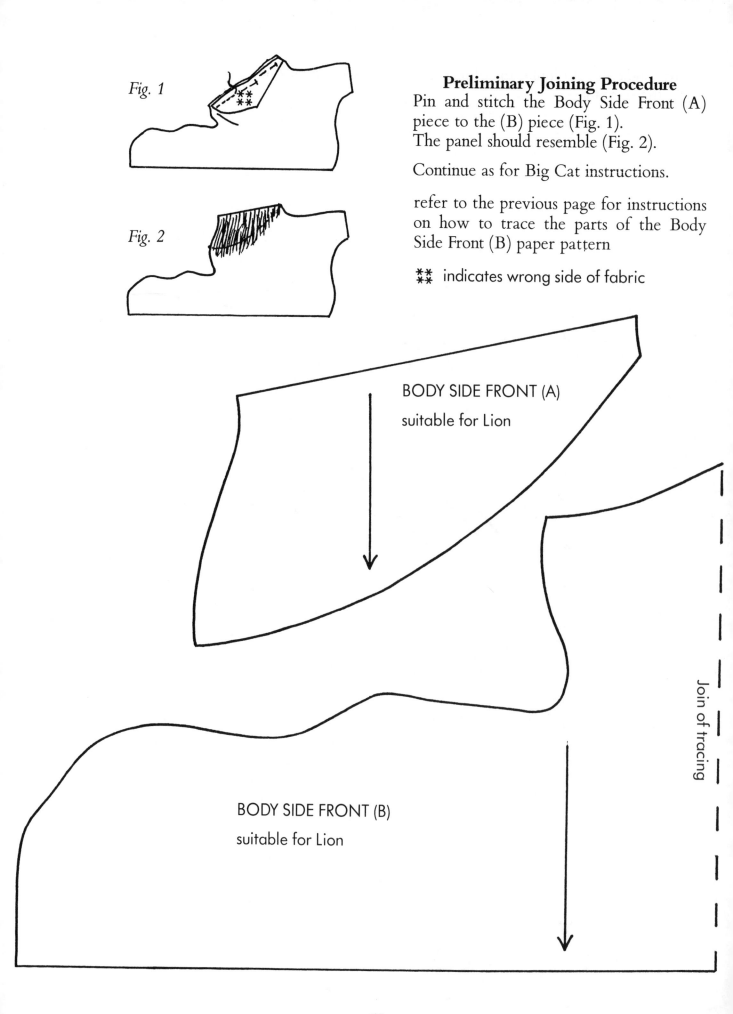

Fig. 1

Fig. 2

Preliminary Joining Procedure
Pin and stitch the Body Side Front (A)
piece to the (B) piece (Fig. 1).
The panel should resemble (Fig. 2).

Continue as for Big Cat instructions.

refer to the previous page for instructions
on how to trace the parts of the Body
Side Front (B) paper pattern

✳✳ indicates wrong side of fabric

BODY SIDE FRONT (A)

suitable for Lion

BODY SIDE FRONT (B)

suitable for Lion

Join of tracing

arrow indicates straight grain of fabric
and stroke of fur

seam allowance 8 mm (⅓″)

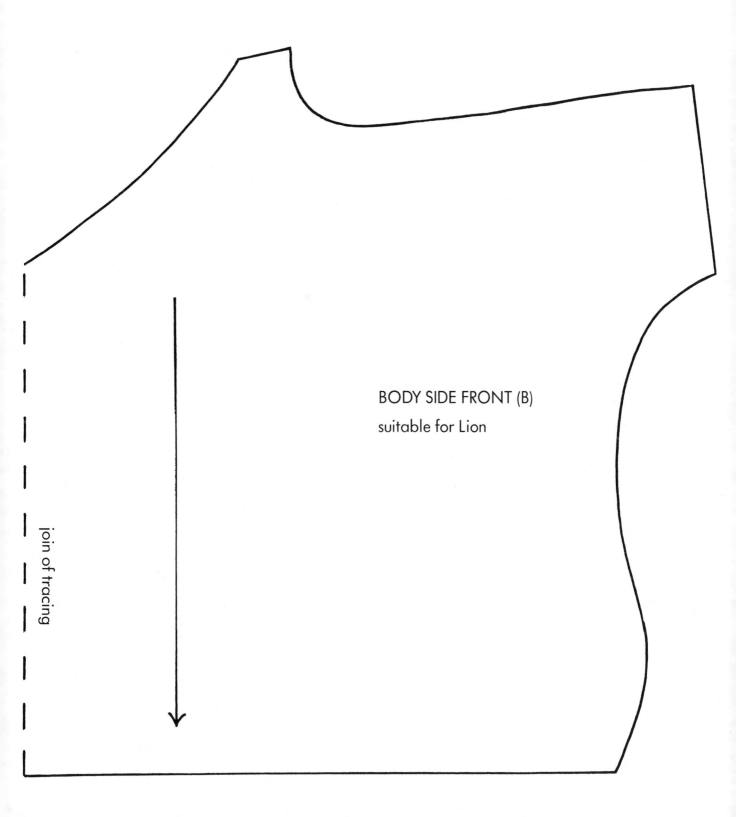

BODY SIDE FRONT (B)

suitable for Lion

join of tracing

seam allowance 8 mm (⅓″)

Step 1:

Step 2:

arrows indicate straight grain of fabric and stroke of fur

To make a paper pattern

Step 1: Trace the Front Gusset piece on to paper.

Step 2: Fold the paper and place it up against a window, so that the light shines through. Transfer the outline and markings onto the other side.

Step 3: Cut out so that the paper pattern resembles the small shape illustrated.

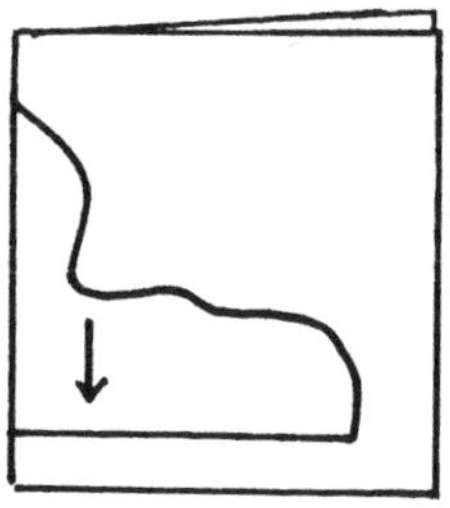

Step 3:

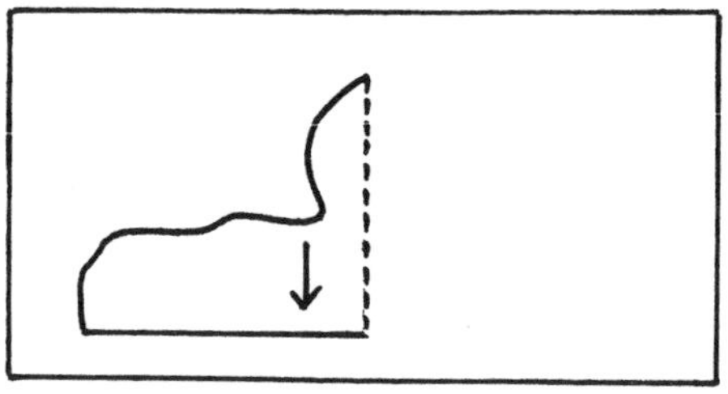

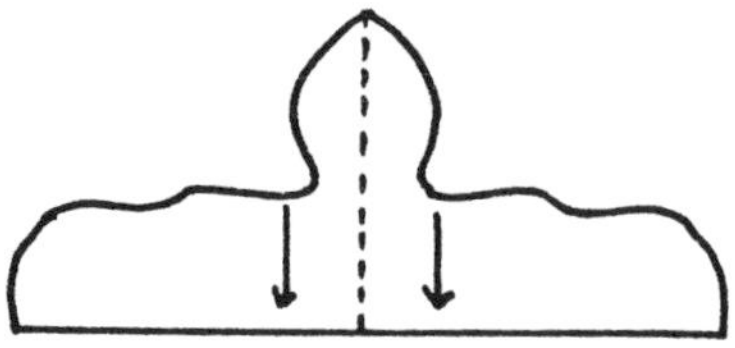

FRONT GUSSET

suitable for Puma, Jaguar, Black Panther, Cheetah, Leopard, Lioness, White Tiger and Tiger

(spot design is suitable for the Cheetah and Leopard)

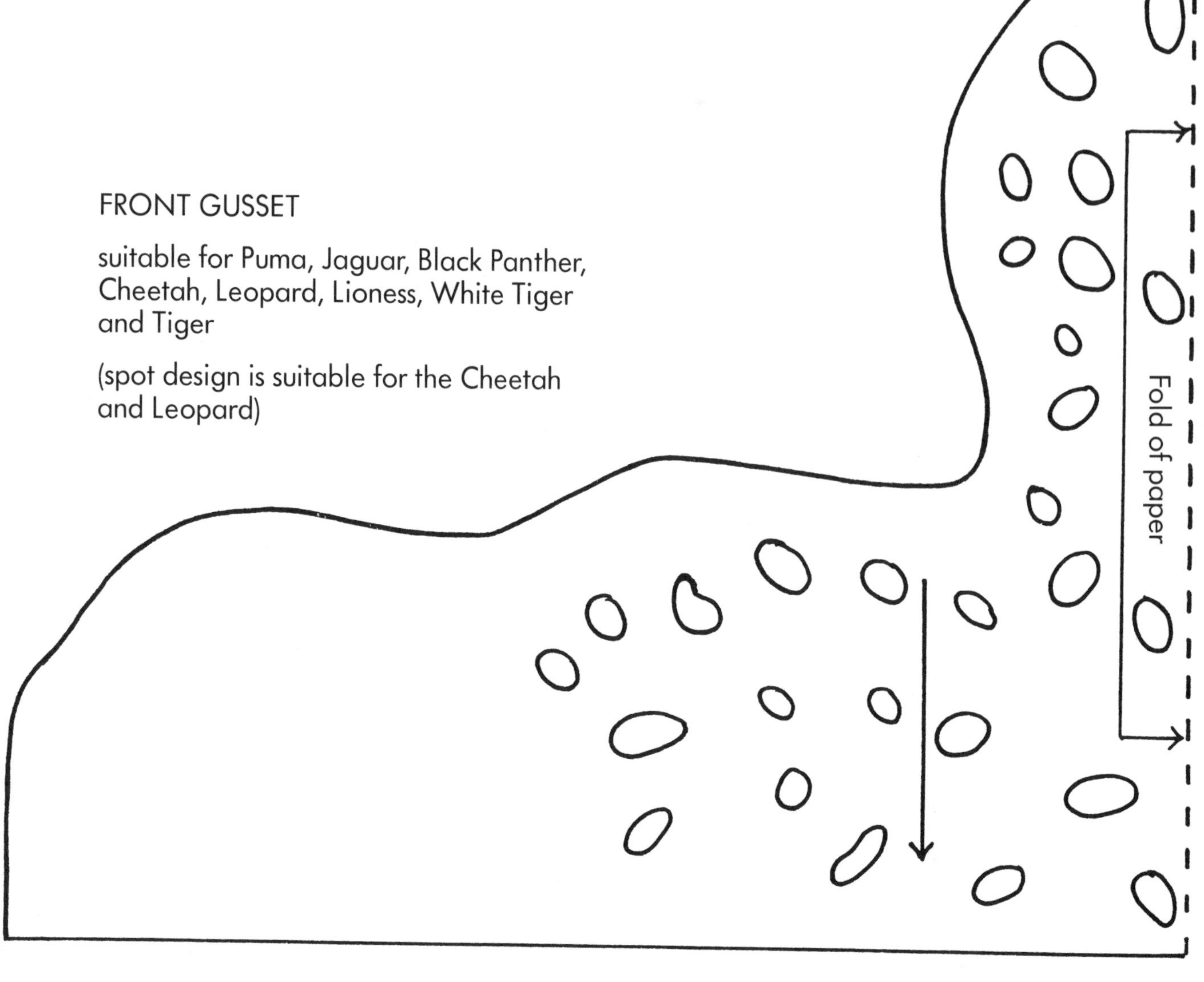

Fold of paper

To make a paper pattern

Step 1: Trace the Front Gusset (D) piece onto paper.

Step 2: Fold the paper, place up against a window and transfer all markings to other side.

Step 3: Cut out.

Step 2

Step 3

F . G .   (D)

Preliminary Joining Procedure

Step 1: Pin and sew a Front Gusset (C) piece to the Front Gusset (D) piece.

Step 2: Sew on the other (C) piece (Fig. 1).

Continue as for the Big Cat instructions.

Fig. 1

✱✱ indicates wrong side of fabric

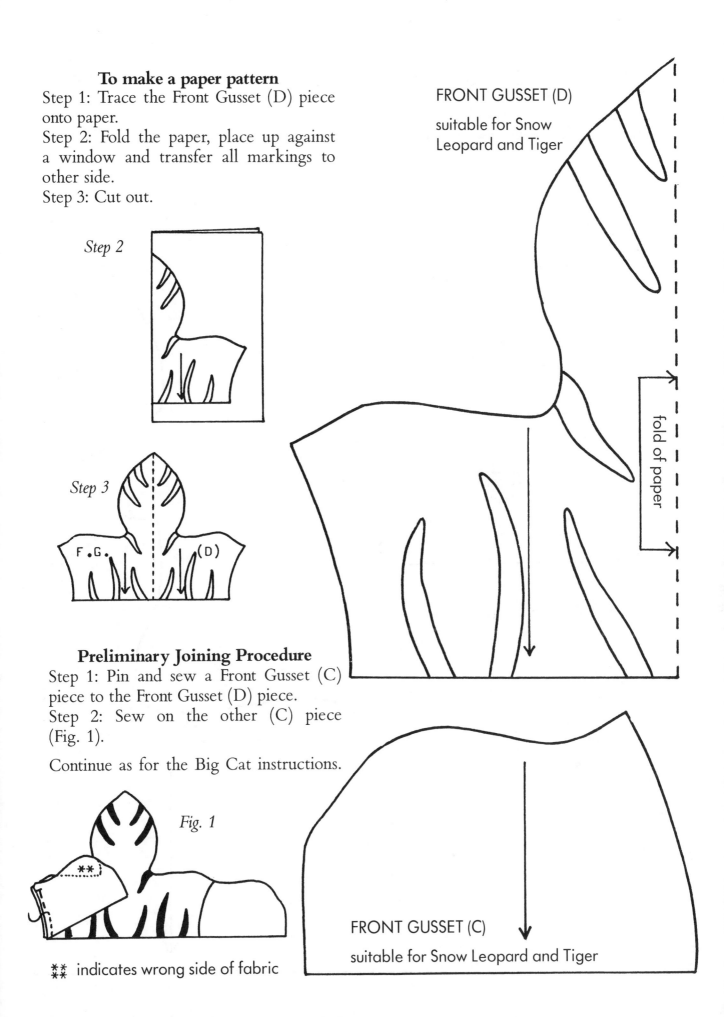

FRONT GUSSET (D)

suitable for Snow Leopard and Tiger

fold of paper

FRONT GUSSET (C)

suitable for Snow Leopard and Tiger

Preliminary Joining Procedure

Step 1: Pin and sew the Front Gusset (A) piece to the (B) piece (Fig. 1) and (Fig. 2). The panel should resemble (Fig. 3).

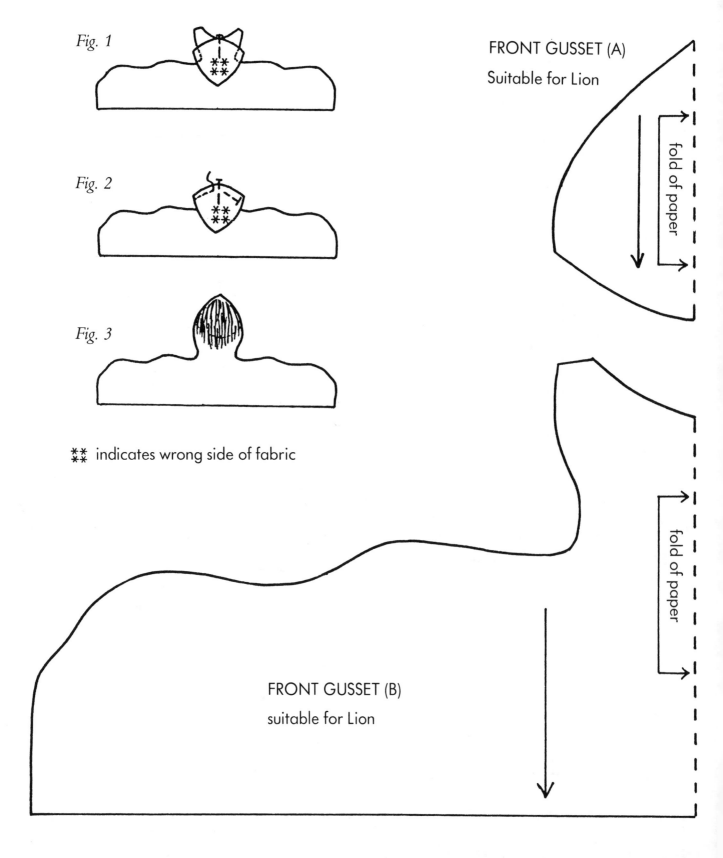

Fig. 1

Fig. 2

Fig. 3

✳✳ indicates wrong side of fabric

FRONT GUSSET (A)

Suitable for Lion

fold of paper

FRONT GUSSET (B)

suitable for Lion

fold of paper

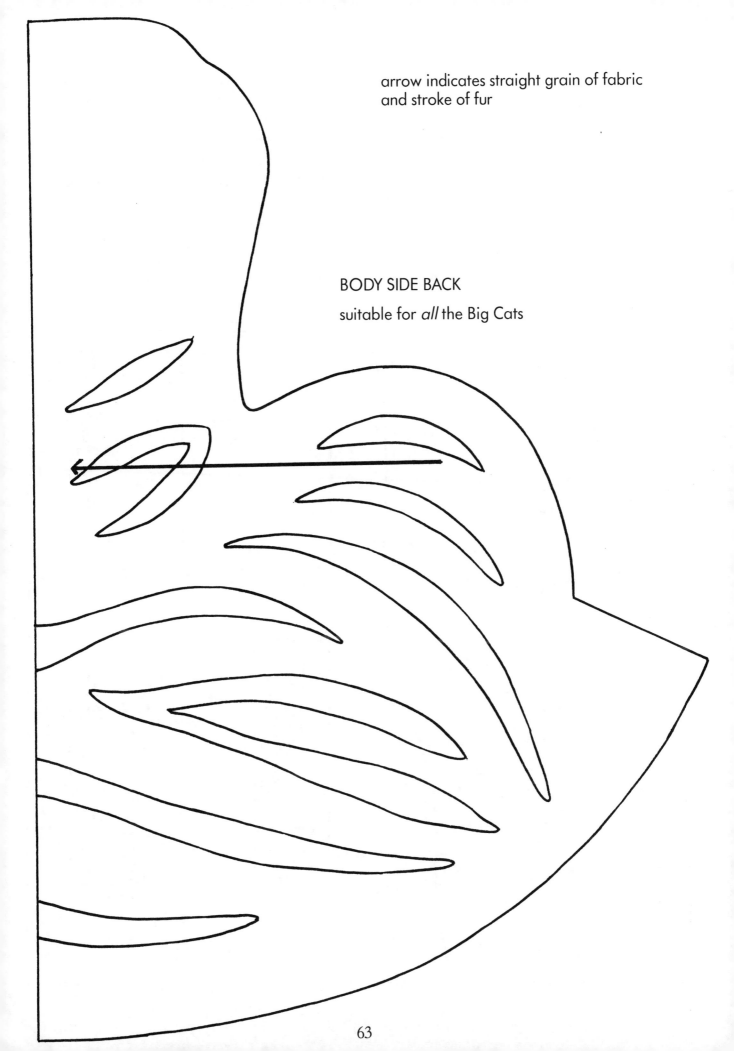

arrow indicates straight grain of fabric
and stroke of fur

BODY SIDE BACK

suitable for *all* the Big Cats

63

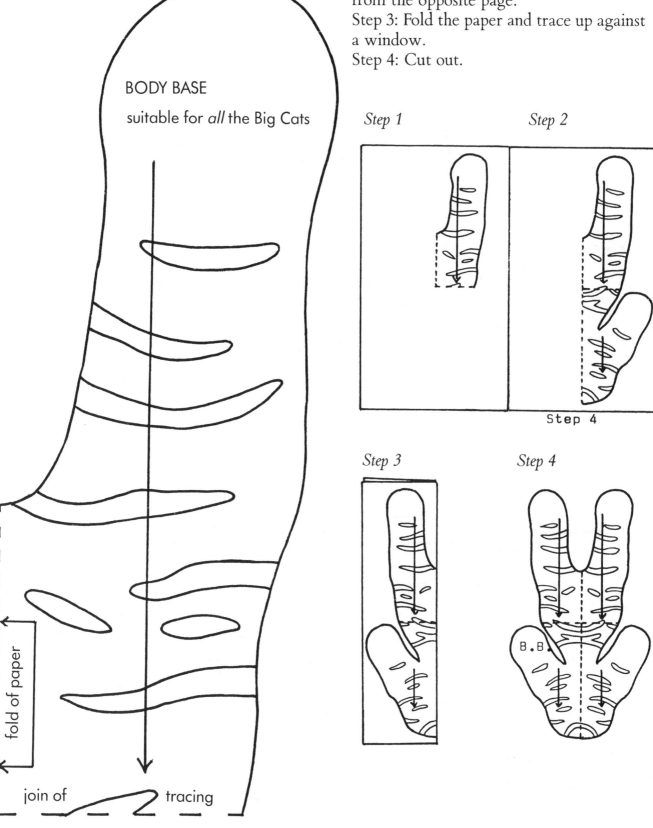

BODY BASE

suitable for *all* the Big Cats

fold of paper

join of   tracing

To make a paper pattern

Step 1: Trace onto paper, the part of the Body Base from this page.

Step 2: Trace the part of the Body Base from the opposite page.

Step 3: Fold the paper and trace up against a window.

Step 4: Cut out.

Step 1

Step 2

Step 4

Step 3

Step 4

B.B.

arrow indicates straight grain of fabric
and stroke of fur

seam allowance 8 mm (⅓″)

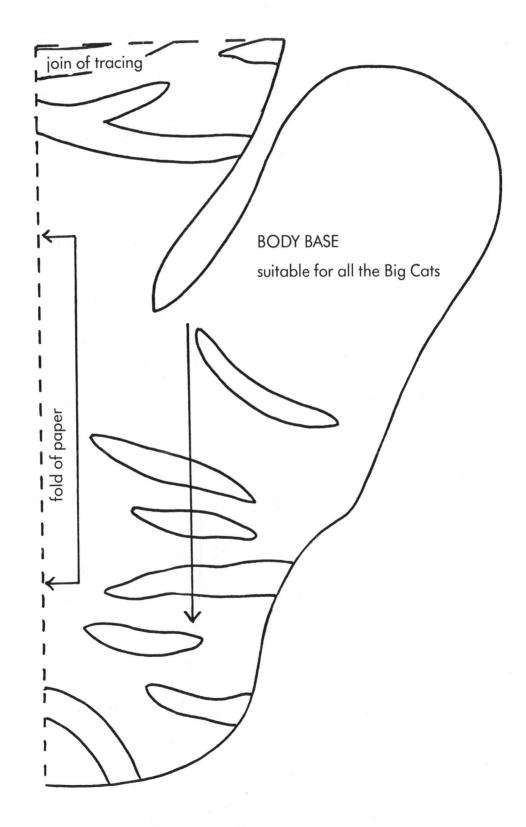

join of tracing

fold of paper

BODY BASE

suitable for all the Big Cats

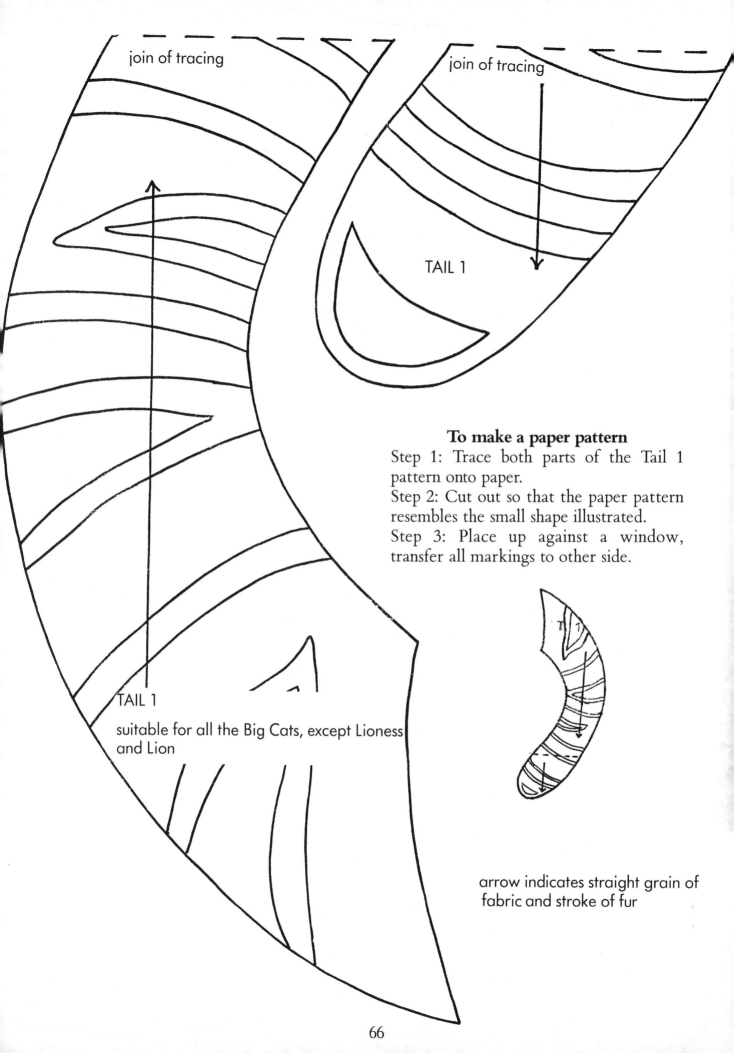

join of tracing

join of tracing

TAIL 1

To make a paper pattern
Step 1: Trace both parts of the Tail 1 pattern onto paper.
Step 2: Cut out so that the paper pattern resembles the small shape illustrated.
Step 3: Place up against a window, transfer all markings to other side.

TAIL 1

suitable for all the Big Cats, except Lioness and Lion

arrow indicates straight grain of fabric and stroke of fur

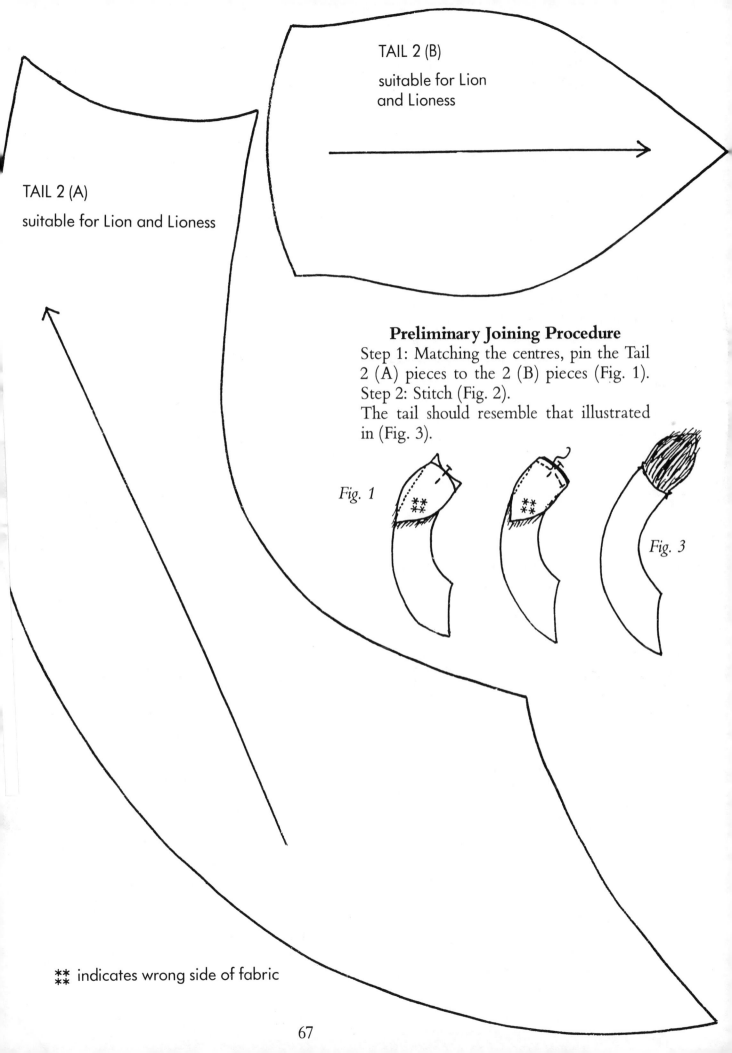

TAIL 2 (B)

suitable for Lion
and Lioness

TAIL 2 (A)

suitable for Lion and Lioness

Preliminary Joining Procedure

Step 1: Matching the centres, pin the Tail 2 (A) pieces to the 2 (B) pieces (Fig. 1).
Step 2: Stitch (Fig. 2).
The tail should resemble that illustrated in (Fig. 3).

Fig. 1

Fig. 3

❋❋ indicates wrong side of fabric

BIG CAT INSTRUCTIONS

METHOD FOR BIG CATS

Ten different big cats can be made from the one set of pattern pieces.

Using the designs provided, such as the Tiger stripes and Cheetah markings, paint your own Big Cat with fabric paint. (Paint all the fabric pieces before sewing.)

The illustrations which accompany the directions on this and the following pages show the Puma, Jaguar, Black Panther, Cheetah and Leopard pattern shapes. However, the methods used to make the toy is the same for all the other, different variations. For the other Big Cats, except the White Tiger, follow the preliminary joining procedure instructions given in the pattern section. Then continue as follows.

Head

1. Pin and stitch the corresponding Head Side Front pieces to the Head Side Back pieces (Fig. 1).

Fig. 1

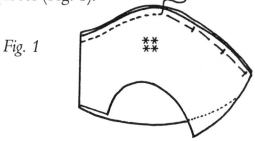

2. Create a centre front neck seam by joining the Head Side Front pieces together (Fig. 2). Tie off all the threads as you work.

Fig. 2

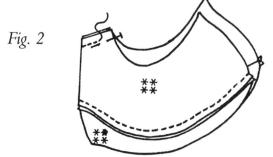

3. Pin and stitch the Cheek pieces together, as shown (Fig. 3).

Fig. 3

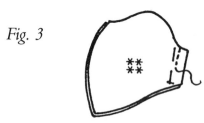

4. To attach the cheeks to the Chin, pin first at the middle, matching the seam to the centre of the narrowest part of the Chin piece, then pin the ends. Next, pin between these pins, easing the fabric as you do so (Fig. 4). Tack by hand, then machine stitch with the Chin piece downwards (Fig. 5). Check the seam from the other side and restitch if necessary.

Fig. 4

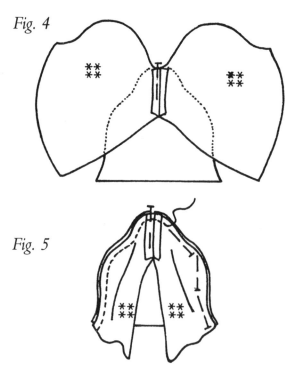

Fig. 5

Note: The tacking is not shown in this or any of the following illustrations.

5. Mark the centre of the straight edge of the Chin piece with a pin. Pin the nose pieces (cheeks and chin) to the head

pieces, matching the pin with the centre front seam (Fig. 6). Tack by hand, then stitch by machine. Check the seam from the other side and restitch, if necessary.

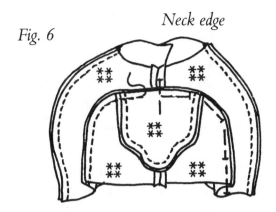

Fig. 6

Neck edge

6. With the right sides together and the wrong side of the Head Gusset piece uppermost, pin the Head Gusset to the head pieces. Match the centre cheek seam with the point of the Head Gusset piece, then pin. Pin the neck edges of the Head Gusset piece to the neck edges of the Head Side Back pieces (Fig. 7). Continue pinning in between these pins, easing the fabric, if necessary.

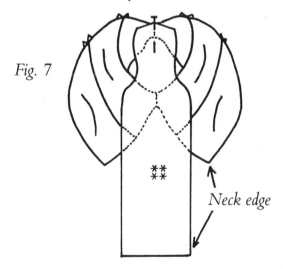

Fig. 7

Neck edge

Machine stitch from the neck edge around to the point of the Head Gusset — the tip of the nose. With the needle in the fabric, lift the presser foot, carefully reposition the fabric and continue stitching around to the other neck edge (Fig. 8). Check the seam from the other side

to make sure that no fabric has been caught in it by mistake. Restitch if necessary if the stitching is too close to the edge. (Tack the nose tip section by hand first if you wish.)

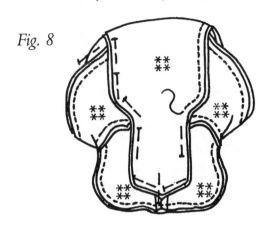

Fig. 8

7. Tie off all threads and clip the curves. Stay stitch the neck opening by sewing with a straight stitch all the way around 2–3 mm (⅛″) away from the edge. Alternatively, whip stitch the edge by hand (Fig. 9).

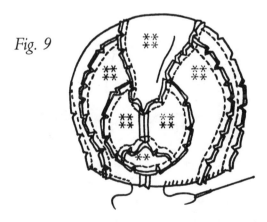

Fig. 9

Note: The stay stitching is not shown in any of the following illustrations.

8. Pin and sew a pair of Ear pieces together. Repeat for the other pair (Fig. 10). Clip the curves, tie off the threads and turn the ears right side out. Stuff loosely so that they are flat not bulky. Turn under 8 mm (⅓″) of fabric along the straight edge and whip stitch the opening closed (Fig. 11).

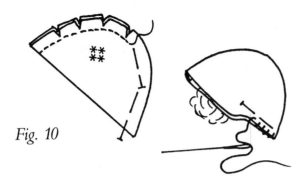

Fig. 10

Note: If using fur fabric, make sure that the fur is tucked in, away from the raw edges, when stitching the seams. For a longer-lasting toy, please heed the advice given in the Hints section (see page 3) concerning the techniques for finishing raw edges.

Note: The Tiger and Snow Leopard ears have the joined Ear 2 (A) and 2 (B) pieces on the back of the ear.

Body

1. Pin and sew the Inside Leg pieces to the Body Side Front pieces (Fig. 1).

Fig. 1

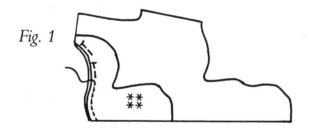

2. Pin and sew the Front Gusset piece to the corresponding Body Side Front piece (Fig. 2). Repeat for the other body side.

Fig. 2

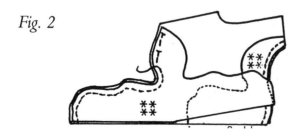

3. Stitch the spine of the body from the neck edge to the straight edge, above the point of the hip (Fig. 3).

Fig. 3

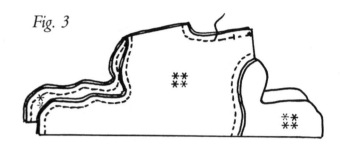

4. Stay stitch the neck opening by sewing with a straight stitch, all the way around 2–3 mm (⅛″) away from the edge. Alternatively, whip stitch the edge by hand.

Fig. 4

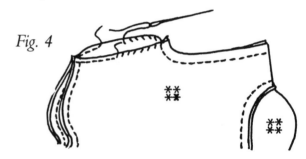

Note: The stay stitching is not shown in any of the following illustrations.

5. Pin and stitch the Body Side Back pieces together (Fig. 5), working from the bottom to the short straight edge.

Fig. 5

6. Matching centre back (spine) seams, pin the Body Side Back pieces to the rest of the body. Stitch from one rear foot all the way over the back to the other rear foot (Fig. 6) and (Fig. 7).

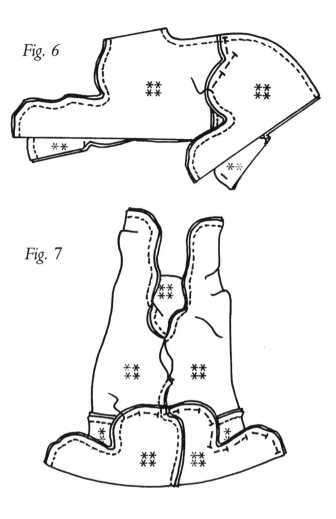

Fig. 6

Fig. 7

9. Match the pins on the Body Base with the seam positions on the body, except for the Front Gusset where it is necessary to match a pin with a pin. Continue pinning between these marked positions until the whole base has been pinned on to the body. The pins should be uppermost as shown in (Fig. 9). Starting anywhere except a tight curve, stitch all the way around. Take care at the seam positions because of the bulk of the fabric. Turn the work over and check the seam from the other side. If the stitching appears irregular, within the seam allowance restitch from the other side (Body Base uppermost) being very careful not to catch any fabric in by mistake.

7. Mark the centre of the straight edge of the Front Gusset with a pin.

8. Mark the Body Base with pins as shown in (Fig. 8). Fold the leg parts of the Body Base in half, lengthways, with the raw edges matching, to find the centre of the paws.

Fig. 9

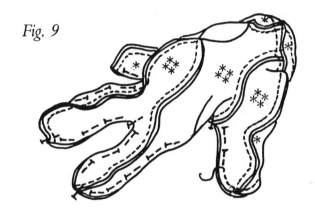

10. Tie off all the threads and clip the curves. Be careful not to cut the stitching (Fig. 10). Turn the body right side out through the neck opening.

Fig. 10

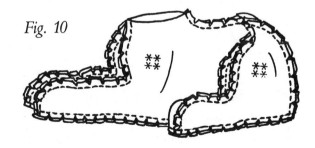

Fig. 8

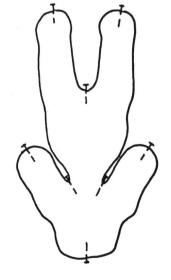

11. Pin and sew the Tail pieces together (Fig. 11). Clip the curves, tie off the threads and turn the tail right side out.

Fig. 11

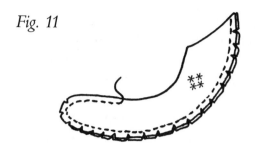

Note: The Tiger tail is made up of two colours. The white (stripes) or white piece is the underneath of the completed tail. Keep this in mind, when completing the toy, sewing on the tail and positioning the head.

Note: Refer to the Hints section (see page 3) for advice on the most successful method of stuffing the toy.

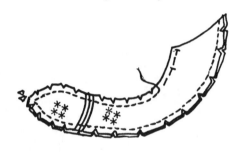

Lion and Lioness only: After sewing the pair of tail sections together, clip the curves. Remember to clip the tail tip also. Turn the tail right side out.

Completing the Toy

1. With the head inside out for fur fabric and either side out for other fabrics, mark the position of the eyes, nose, ears and whiskers. To assist in marking the whiskers, make a template by tracing the Cheek pattern and markings onto paper or thin card. Trim off the 8 mm (⅓″) seam allowance all the way around. Poke holes through the template where marked with a needle. Mark the whisker positions through the holes onto the fabric with a sharp tailor's chalk pencil or a non-permanent fabric marker (Fig. 1).

Fig. 1

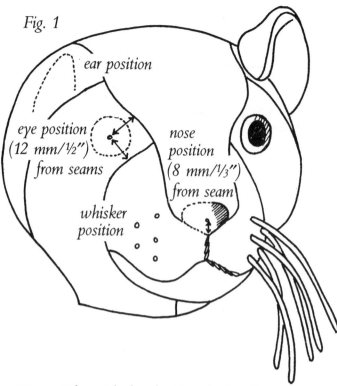

ear position

eye position (12 mm/½″) from seams

nose position (8 mm/⅓″) from seam

whisker position

Note: *The right-hand side of the illustration shows what the features will look like on the completed, stuffed toy.*

2. With a stitch ripper/unpicker, cut through a couple of threads in the fabric where the eye position is marked. Carefully push the shank of the 'safety' eye through the hole, gently enlarging it as you do so. Repeat the procedure with the other eye; check to make sure that the eyes look even and not lopsided. Press a washer down firmly onto each shank (Fig. 2), having the curved points of the washer uppermost. The fabric is trapped between the eye on the outside and the washer on the inside (Fig. 3).

Fig. 2   *Fig. 3*

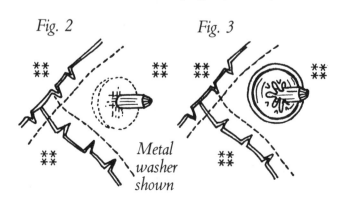

Metal washer shown

3. Following the same procedure as for the eyes, attach the 'safety' nose. Alternatively, embroider the nose on with satin stitch, after the head has been attached to the body.

4. Make the whiskers in the following way: Thread a length of hat elastic onto an upholstery needle or a needle with a large eye. Tie a knot in the end of the elastic, then knot over the first knot a couple of times so that it becomes larger. With the knot on the inside of the head, sew through to the outside where a whisker position has been marked. Without unthreading the needle, cut the elastic so that 7.5 cm (3″) protrudes from the cheek. Repeat the procedure for the other whiskers (Fig. 1). If fur fabric is being used, it may be necessary to leave a 'tail' on the elastic so that the ends can be tied together on the inside of the head to prevent the whiskers being pulled out. Make the 'tail' about 4 cm (1½″) long by tying the knot further away from the end of the elastic. Make sure that when the 'tails' are tied together the cheek remains flat and is not puckered. Give the whisker a little tug to make the knot sit flush with the fabric (Fig. 4).

Fig. 4

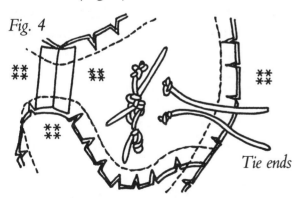

Tie ends

5. Join the head to the body.

Method A — Leave the body wrong side out. Turn the head right side out. Insert the head into the neck opening of the body, so that the raw edges of the neck openings are even. Match the centre chin seam with the point of the Front Gusset or have it slightly to one side. Pin the edges together, around the inside of the neck opening. Stitch 8 mm (⅓″) from the edge so that an opening is left at the back of the toy, 5 cm (2″) long, to allow for turning. Stitch again for strength. Turn the toy right side out through the opening. Stuff firmly. (See the Hints section on page 3.) Using ladder stitch, sew the opening closed, adding a little more stuffing to make the neck firmer (Fig. 5). Sew again for strength.

Fig. 5

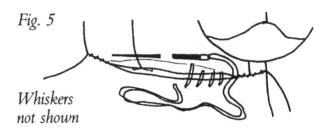

Whiskers not shown

Method B — Turn the head and the body right side out. Stuff firmly. Position the head so that it looks straight ahead or slightly to one side. Using ladder stitch and a strong doubled thread, sew the head to the body leaving an opening 5 cm (2″) long at the back or side of the toy. Add more stuffing to make the neck firmer and sew closed. Stitch all the way around again for strength (Fig. 5).

6. Using ladder stitch, attach the ears to the head, where marked.

Note: Use pins to mark the position of the ears if using fur fabric. Stitch to the point of the 'v'-shaped marking (Fig. 6), then fold the ear flat onto the head and continue stitching. Restitch for strength, sewing the inside curve of the ear also, if possible (Fig. 7).

Fig. 6   Fig. 7

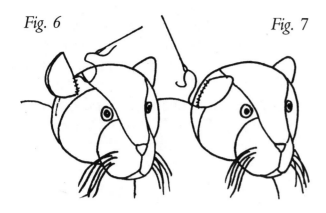

7. Stuff the tail firmly. Position the tail to curve to either side of the body — preferably, if the head is looking to one side, the tail should curve to the same side. Ladder stitch the tail in position (Fig. 8) using a strong doubled thread. Leaving an opening of 5 cm (2″), add more stuffing, then stitch the opening closed. Stitch around again for strength.

Fig. 8

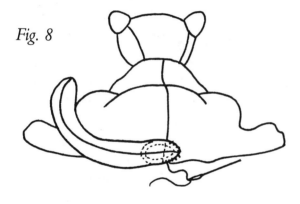

8. Using 6 strands of embroidery floss, stem/outline stitch a mouth as illustrated (Fig. 1). Stitching over the seam, sew only halfway along the length of the cheek/chin seam.

Note: For a toy made from fur fabric simplify the mouth, having three long stitches visible instead.

9. Using 6 strands of embroidery floss, create toes on each paw (except for fur fabric toy). Hiding the knot in the seam, make three stitches 2.5 cm (1″) long, 2 cm (¾″) apart. Making the centre stitch cover the seam, pull each stitch a little as you sew to give the toes shape (Fig. 9).

Fig. 9

Note: If necessary, slightly trim the fur from around the eyes and nose. Run the blunt end of a needle along the seams to pluck out any trapped fur. (Try not to catch the threads of the backing.) Comb the toy. Only a small amount of fluff should come out.

10. To keep the ends of the elastic whiskers looking neat, paint them with clear nail polish.